DERRY IN 1688

REPRINT

OF

WALKER'S

Diary of the Siege of Derry,

IN 1688-89.

A TRUE

ACCOUNT

OF THE

SIEGE

OF

London-Derry.

By the Reverend Mr. *George Walker*, Rector of *Donoghmoore* in the County of *Tirone*, and late Governour of *Derry* in *Ireland*.

The Second Edition Corrected.

The Naval & Military Press Ltd

Published by

The Naval & Military Press Ltd

Unit 5 Riverside, Brambleside
Bellbrook Industrial Estate
Uckfield, East Sussex
TN22 1QQ England

Tel: +44 (0)1825 749494

www.naval-military-press.com
www.nmarchive.com

Licenſed,

BY Command of the Right Honourable the Earl of *Shrewsbury*, Principal Secretary of State.

J. Vernon.

Sept. 13.
  1689.

May it please Your Majesties,

NExt to the Pleasure of doing well, there is no greater satisfaction than where the Performance meets with a favourable reception from those for whose sake it is designed. I thank God I have this double Comfort in the Testimony of a good Conscience, and Your Majesties Gracious Acceptance of the poor services God enabled me to doe for your Majesties Interest, and the Safety of those Protestants, whom the Fury of the *Papists* drove into *London-Derry.*

Nor am I more pleased with Your Majesties Royal Bounty to me, much above not only my Merit, but Expectation, than with Your Majesties Tenderness for my Poor Fellow Sufferers and Partners in that Action, whom I doubt not but Your Majesties will find as brave in the Field, and in taking other Towns, as in defending that, which neither the Number, nor Rage of their Enemies without, nor those more cruel Ones within, of Famine and Sickness, could ever make them think of Surrendring. The Part I Acted in
this

this Service might more properly have been done by other hands; but that Necessity which threw it upon me, will I hope justifie me before God and the World, from the irregularity of interesting my self in such an Affair, for which I was neither by Education or Function qualified; Especially since the necessity which called me to it, was no sooner over, than I resigned more chearfully than ever I undertook the Employment, that I might apply my self to the Plow to which I had put my Hand. I am not at all angry with the Reflexions that some make, as they think, to my Disparagement; because all they say of this kind, gives God the greater Honour, in whose Almighty Hand no instrument is weak, in whose Presence no Flesh must glory. But as the whole Conduct of this matter must be ascribed to Providence alone, as it ought, this should then give them occasion to consider that God has Espoused your Majesties Cause, and Fights your Battels, and for the Protestant Religion; and by making use of a poor Minister, the unworthiest of the whole Communion, of which he is a Member, would intimate to the World, by what Hand he will defend and maintain both your Majesties Interest, and the Religion you have delivered from those that were ready to swallow both up.

That

The Epistle Dedicatory.

That which I here presume to lay at Your Majesties Feet, is indeed very unfit for Your Royal View ; but that since Importunity would have it publick, I thought it Sacrilege to entitle any other to the Copy, than those to whom the Original was devoted. The Picture cannot be commended for the Workmanship, but it may possibly be the more acceptable, for that because more resembling the Life from which 'tis drawn : There is little Skill, or Art, in either, but there are Ornaments much more valuable in both, natural Simplicity, Sincerity, and a plain Truth, In which character I humbly beg your Majesties will always consider, and accept of the Endeavours of

> Your Majesties most Obliged,
>> Most Faithfull, and most Obedient
>> Subject and Servant,

>>> *George Walker.*

PREFACE TO THE FOURTH EDITION.

WITHIN the short period of three years the Publisher has been called upon to issue another and fourth edition of "Walker's Diary of the Siege of Derry." It is now presented in a different and improved shape and type from the others which were previously issued, but the same scrupulous care has been observed to present every word as spelled and written in the original edition, published under the supervision of its renowned Author, and to make the present History an exact copy of the work printed in 1689, so far as it possibly could be done. The Publisher felt that a veracious and reliable record of the noble defence of Derry was desirable in the absence of such as accurately described the transactions of the Siege, and he believed that none was so likely to be regarded in that light as that one which came from the pen of the great central figure and leader in the struggle. That he did not miscalculate the public mind is proved by the fact that he is again called upon to commit

a

Preface to the Fourth Edition.

a new edition to the press, and he hopes that
the typography and style of the present
volume may find an equally favourable reception with those which have preceded it. The
three former editions are exhausted, and, as
the Publisher is frequently called upon for
" The History of the Siege of Derry " both
from at home and abroad, he hopes his desire
to gratify the patriotic feeling may be regarded
as successful in the present edition.

Derry, January, 1895.

A Description of the CITY of
London-Derry.

THE Form of the Town comes somewhat
near an *Oblong* or long Square ; and its
Situation lengthways, is *N. W.* and *S. E.* or a
Diagonal drawn from the Church through the
Market-house, to the Magazine, is near upon
a *N.* and *S.* Line.

The Length of the Town through the middle from *Ship-key gate to Bishops-gate*, is about
300 Paces, or 1500 Feet.   The Wall on the
W. side the Town 320 Paces ; the Wall on
the *E.* about 380.

The Breadth at the *N. W.* End 140 ; at the
S. E. End 120 ; from *Butchers-gate to Ferry-
key-gate*, where the Town is Broadest, 180
Paces.

The Wall is generally 7 or 8 Foot thick ;
but the out-side Wall of Stone, or Battlements
above the *Terra-plene*, is not more than two
Foot in thickness.

The Four Corners have each of them a
Bastion ; on the long side to the *West*-ward
are two other Bastions ; and on the side to
the *East*-ward, one Bastion, one Demi-bas-
tion, and two other Works which are commonly call'd Flat-forms.

There are four Gates ; *Bishops-gate* at the
S. E. End, *Ship-key-gate* at the end opposite
to

to it : *Butchers-gate* at the *N. E.* Side, and *Ferry-key-gate* over against it.

In the middle of the Town is a *Square*, call'd the *Diamond :* where the *Market-House* stands (during the Siege, turned into a *Guard-House.*)

Near the *S. W.* end of the town, stands the Church ; on the top whereof, being a flat Roof, were placed two of our Guns, which were of great Use in annoying the Enemy. In the *S. E.* Angle of the Town, was the principal Magazine, within the Town also were several Wells, &c. and before *Bishops-gate* was a *Ravelin* built by Col. *Lundy* ; and the Ground on Forwards to the *Wind-mill-hill,* was taken in by the Besieged to the Distance of 260 Paces from the Town, and about the same Distance a cross from the River ; and for fear this Ground should be taken from the Besieged by the Enemy, another Line was industriously drawn from the *S. W.* Quarter of the Town, to the River, to secure their Retreat.

The Number of Guns planted on the Bastions and Lines, was 8 *Sakers* and 12 *Demi-culverins.*

The whole Town stands upon an easy Ascent, and exposed most of the Houses to the Enemies Guns.

A Diary of the SIEGE of
LONDON-DERRY.

BEing prevail'd on, to give an Account of
the Siege of *London-Derry*, it is convenient, by way of preliminary, to take notice
how that Town came to be out of the Hands
of the *Irish*, when all places of the Kingdom
of any strength or consideration were possessed by them. It pleased God so to
infatuate the Councils of my Lord *Tyrconnel*,
that when the three Thousand Men were sent
to *England* to assist his Master against the
Invasion of the Prince of *Orange*, he took particular care to send away the whole Regiment
Quartered in and about this City ; he soon
saw his Error, and endeavoured to repair it,
by Commanding my Lord *Antrim* to Quarter
there with his Regiment, consisting of a
numerous swarm of *Irish* and *Highlanders ;*
upon the 6*th.* of *December*, they were on their
March in and about *New Town* (a Market-
Town belonging to Col. *George Philips*, 12
Miles distant from *Derry*) Col. *Philips* having
notice of this, and joining with it the appre-
hensions they were under, of a general Insurrection of the *Irish* intended on the 9*th* of
December, and considering that *Derry* as well
as other places was to be presently possessed
by

by the *Irish*, and having several Informations
brought him, and some taken before him that
gave some credit to the Fear and Jealousies
they were under, and encreased his suspicion
of some damnable Design against the *British*
of those parts ; He immediately dispatches a
Letter to Alderman *Norman*, giving an Account
of these Matters, and his Opinion of them,
and importuning him to consult with the
sober People of the Town, and to set out the
Danger of admitting such Guests among
them : The next day he sent an Express,
advising him to cause the Gates of the City
to be shut, and assured them he would be
with them with his Friends the day following,
and would stand by them and would serve
them to the hazard of his Life and Fortune.
Alderman *Norman* and the rest of the graver
Citizens were under great Disorder and Con-
sternation, and knew not what to resolve
upon. One of the Companies was already in
view of the Town, and two of the Officers
within it, but the younger sort who are
seldom so dilatory in their Resolutions, got
together, run in all hast to the Main-Guard,
snatcht up the Keys, and immediately shut
up all the Four-Gates, and the Magazine. On
the 9*th* day, Col *Philips* comes into *London-
derry*, he had been Governour of that Town,
as also of the Fort of *Culmore* in King
Charles's

Charles's time, and therefore the Inhabitants desire him to resume the Government, and immediately delivered him the Keys of the Gates, and the Magazine : He being well acquainted with proceedings in *England*, with the advice of the Gravest sort, dispatches Mr. *David Kerns* as their Agent thither, to represent their Condition and Resolutions, and to procure some speedy relief.

News being carried to *Dublin* of this Revolt, as they call'd it, the Lord *Montjoy* with his Lieutenant-Collonel *Lundy* and six Companies, are sent down to reduce the Place. The Governour had already form'd Eight Companies of good effectual Men in the City, and Armed them out of the Stores, and with some Management, quieted all Factions and Tumults, and reduced all things to good Order, so that all were Unanimously resolved to stand it out till they received a Return to their Address sent into *England*. My Lord *Montjoy* appears before the Town ; his interest among us, and the consideration of our own Circumstances, that there was no appearance of any sudden Relief from *England*, no Provisions in the Town, and (which was worst of all) but two Barrels of Powder in the Magazine, which my Lord *Montjoy* must needs understand, being Master of the Ordnance ; made it thought most
adviseable

adviseable to listen to a Treaty; so the
Governour, with the Consent of the City-
Council agreed upon certain Capitulations;
that only two Companies should enter the
Town, and they to be all Protestants, and
that the Town Companies should be allow'd
to keep their Arms and to do duty with the
others, & that no stranger is to be admitted
into the City, without License from the
Governour and Sheriffs. Having obtained
Conditions of so easy a Nature, and of so
probable Advantage to the Town, they receiv'd my Lord *Montjoy*, who made Lieutenant-Collonel *Lundy*, Governour of the
Town.

The Gentlemen of the other parts of the
North of *Ireland*, being well acquainted with
the Proceedings at *Dublin*: that particularly,
Commissions were given out to raise many
Thousands of *Irish*, all over the Kingdom;
and all to be Maintained at the Expense of
their Officers (who were not able to Support
themselves) for the space of three Months.
They were with good reason equally apprehensive, this was not intended for their
Safety or Advantage; and therefore they
generally resolved to put themselves in the
best Posture they could to Defend themselves
against any inconveniences such Methods
might bring upon them: They had several
Consultations

Consultations with their Neighbours, and some Great Men were not wanting in their Advice and Encouragement. One left some Instructions with Mr. *George Walker* Rector of *Donaghmore* in the County of *Tyrone*, recommending the necessity of Securing *Dungannon* by a Garrison of their own, and of Victualling that Town ; in order to which, Mr. *Walker* saw it not only excuseable, but necessary to concern himself, and raise **Men**, out of which he form'd a Regiment, and to apply what Interest he could make towards the Preservation of that Town. *Gordon O'Neale*, observing those Preparations, sends his Priest to inquire into the meaning of them, which was readily interpreted to him ; *So many* Irish *were Arm'd in the Country, they thought fit to put themselves in a Posture of Defence against the Danger they saw themselves exposed to.* The Men complained of want of Powder, but by the Contrivance of their Officer, a Bag of *Mustard-Seed* was laid upon the Carriages, which by its resemblance, easily obtained the Credit of a Bag of Powder, and immediately gave motion to the Souldiers.

In order to settle a Correspondence with *London-Derry*, Mr. *Walker* Rides to that Town, and Consults Collonel *Lundy*. The Opinion they had of his Experience in **War**,

and

and Zeal for the Cause they were to Maintain, gave all People great Expectation from his Conduct; he Approves and Encourages the Design, sends two Files of his Disciplin'd Men to *Dungannon*, and afterwards two Troops of Dragoons.

March 14. Orders were sent to Col. *Steward*, (who was very considerable among us), from Col. *Lundy*, that the Garrison at *Dungannon* should break up; some considering the advantagious situation of the place, and the great quantity of Provisions already laid in, and the consequence of leaving both, to give strength to their Enemies, shew'd some unwillingness to comply with Commands so different from the Measures they had hitherto pursued; but at last, agreed to March to *Colrain* or *Derry* according to Collonel *Lundy's* Orders.

March 17. We March'd as far as *Strabane*, and there met our Order from Collonel *Lundy* to return to *Omagh* and the *Rash*. Five Companies of the above Regiment are Quartered at *Rash*, under Command of Mr. *Walker*; and five at *Omagh*, Commanded by Lieutenant-Collonel *Mervin*: A Fortnight after, we receiv'd a Potent to March to *St. Johnstown*, five Miles from *Derry*.

March 20. Captain *James Hamilton* arrived from *England*, with Ammunition and Arms,

Arms, 480 Barrels of Powder, and Arms for 2000 Men, and a Commission from the King and Queen for Col. *Lundy* to be Governour of the City, together with Instructions to swear all Officers Military and Civil, and assurance of speedy Supplies from *England*. The King and Queen are publickly Proclaimed with great Joy and Solemnity. About this time the *Irish* made a descent into *Ulster*, and drove great Numbers of poor Protestants before them, who took shelter in *Colrain* and *London-Derry*.

March 23. Col. *Philips* is sent to *England* with an Address to the King, and to Sollicit a speedy Supply.

Col. *Lundy* goes to *Colrain* to give his Advice and Assistance to that place. The rest of this Month, and the beginning of the next, is spent in Preparations against the Enemy; they had possessed themselves of *Colrain*, & drove all before them till they came to *Clody*-Bridge, of which I shall give this short Account.

April 13. Mr. *Walker* receiving Intelligence, that the Enemy was drawing towards *Derry*, he Rides in all hast thither, and gives Col. *Lundy* an Account of it, but the Collonel believed it only a false Alarm; Mr. *Walker* returns from him to *Lyfford*, where he joined Col. *R. Crofton;* the Enemy come
to

to *Clody-ford;* all Night long the Enemy
and We fired at one another, and in the
Morning, Mr. *Walker* took his Post at the
long Cawsey as Commanded by Col. *Lundy,*
leaving Col. *Crofton* to maintain the Post
against the Enemy, which he performed with
good Resolution.

The Souldiers having spent all their Ammunition, *viz.* three Charges of Powder a
man, are forced to give way ; Major *Stroud*
rallies the Horse in order to bring off the
Foot : The Regiment at the *Long-Cawsy* was
in some danger, having staid too long, ex-
pecting Orders, but got off under the shelter
of some Horse, & following the Army, which
was 10000 strong, and make good their
Retreat to *Derry* ; Col. *Lundy* and several of
Quality being then at the Head of them.
Mr. *Walker* found the Gates shut against
him and his Regiment, and staid all Night
without the Gates ; next day with much
difficulty and some violence upon the Centry
they got in : Mr. *Walker* waited on Col.
Lundy, and press'd the taking the Field ; but
he not being satisfied with the behaviour of
his Army the day before, gave Advice of a
different Nature, which did not agree with
Mr. *Walkers* Sentiments, who thought himself obliged to stand by his men that he had
brought from their own homes, and not to
Expose

Expose them again to the Enemy, by dismissing them.

April 15.   Col. *Cunningham* and Col. *Richards* came into the Lough from *England*, with two Regiments and other Necessaries for Supply of *Derry.*

There were several remarkable Passages might be here inserted, relating to those that came from *Drumore* and *Colrain ;* but as I would not reproach any, so I cannot do right to all ; and whatever mis-fortune the difficulty of those places brought upon them, the behaviour of such of them as staid in the Garrison of *Derry*, sets them above Apologys for any miscarriage ; for certainly there could not be better Men in the World ; and many of those that left us, have been exposed to Censure ; but I hope the World will be so just, not to give Characters from things done in such a confusion.

April 17. Upon the News of King *James's* Army being on their March towards *Londonderry*, Colonel *Lundy*, our Governour, thought fit to call a Councel ; and that Col. *Cuningham*, and Col. *Richards*, that were sent from *England*, to our Assistance, should be Members of it ; accordingly they met, and with other Gentlemen equally unacquainted with the Condition of the Town, or the Inclination and Resolution of the People, they make this following Order.   *Upon*

Upon inquiry it appears, That there is not Provision in the Garrison of London-derry, *for the present Garrison, and the two Reigments on Board, for above a Week, or Ten Days at most, and it appearing that the Place is not tenable against a well-appointed Army : Therefore it is concluded upon, and resolv'd, That it is not convenient for His Majesty's Service, but the contrary, to land the two Regiments under Col. Cuningham & Col. Richards, their Command now on Board in the River of Lough foyle. That considering the present Circumstances of Affairs, & the likelihood the Enemy will soon possess themselves of this Place, it is thought most convenient, that the principal Officers shall privately withdraw themselves, as well for their own preservation, as in hopes that the Inhabitants, by a timely Capitulation, may make terms the better with the Enemy ; and that this we Judge most convenient for His Majesty's Service, as the present State of Affairs now is.*

After this Resolution, an Instrument was prepar'd to be Subscribed by the Gentlemen of the Councel, and to be sent to King *James,* who was advanced in Person with his Army as far as St. *John's* Town ; it was recommended with this Encouragement ; *There was no doubt, but upon surrender of the Town, King* James *would Grant a General Pardon, and Order Restitution of all that had been Plunder'd from them.* Some Gentlemen were influenced by these considerations to subscribe

subscribe, others did not only refuse but
began to conceive some Jealousies of their
Governour ; and some, tho' they did but
guess at their proceedings, express'd themselves after a ruder manner, threatening to
hang both the Governour and his Council.
Captain *White* is sent out to the King. to
receive proposals from him ; and it was at
the same time agreed with Lieutenant
General *Hamilton*, that he should not march
the Army within four Miles of the Town.

Notwithstanding which, King *James* having
some confidence given him, that the Town,
upon his Majesties approach, would un-
doubtedly surrender to him, and that the
very sight of so formidable an army would
fright them into a Compliance : Upon the
18*th* of *April* advances, with his Army, before
our Walls, with Flying Colours ; His Majesty
thinking it discretion, to use the shelter of a
Party of Horse on South-end of *Derry*-hill,
the more safely to observe what salutation
His Forces had from the Garrison.

Orders were given, that none should dare
to fire till the King's Demands were first
known, by another Messenger to be sent to
His Majesty for that purpose ; but our men
on the Walls, wondering to see Lieut. Gen.
Hamilton (contrary to his Engagement, not
to come within four Miles of the Town)
approaching

approaching our Walls in such order, they imagining they were by some means or other betray'd, thought it reasonable to consider their own safety, and to keep the Enemy at distance, by firing their Guns upon them, which they accordingly did.

The Enemy that were great strangers to this sort of exercise, upon this could not be kept in any order by their Officers, but soon took to their heels, others with less Labour could hide themselves, and a great many were kill'd. King *James* did shew himself in some disorder, and much surprised to find the behaviour of his Army, as well as of the Besieged, so different from the character he had receiv'd of both ; some were apprehensive of the King's displeasure upon such a disappointment, and sent Arch-Deacon *Hamilton*, and Mr. *Nevil*, to beg His Majesties pardon for having drawn His Majesty into so dangerous and unsuccessful an undertaking, and to signify to him the difficulty of commanding or perswading so tumultuous and untractable a Rabble, to any moderation or complyance ; but if His Majesty drew off his Army, till those Gentlemen return'd, and brought assurance of His Majesty's presence with it (of which some question was yet made) they doubted not but they could bring them to a better understanding.

This

This evening King *James* retired with his Army to St. *Johns* Town. In the mean time Mr. *Muckcridge*, the Town-Clark, sees it absolutely necessary, to give some intimation of Proceedings at the Council of War, which (tho' every man's concern) care was taken not to make too publick, *viz.* That Colonel *Cuningham*, his Ships, Men, and Provision should return to *England*, and all Gentlemen and others in Arms should quit the Garrison, and goe along with him : this discovery occasion'd great uneasiness and disorder in the Town, which had like to have had very ill effects upon the Governour and some of his Council ; it did also add much to the rage and violence of the Garrison, when they heard some wrong had been done my Lord *Kingston* and his Party, by the indirect measures of some within our Walls, their concern for him being as great as their expectations from him.

The Governour and his Council finding themselves of little interest in the Town, and that they could not be further serviceable, &c. thought fit to retire, and not to press the matter further. Some of the Gentlemen left us in all this confusion, and made their escape to the Ships at *Kilmore*, tho' not without some hazard ; for the Souldiers were under great discontent, to find themselves
deserted

deserted by those that engaged them in the difficulties they were then under, and were not easily kept from expressing it with violence upon some Persons; but it was the care of others to keep them in temper, and from those outrages, as well as to support them against such discouragements.

Sir *Arthur Royden* protested against the proceedings of the Council, and would not have left the Town, but that he was dangerously sick, and was forc'd from us by the advice of his Physitian and Friends.

Governour *Lundy* could not so easily make his escape, being conceived more obnoxious than any of the rest, but found it convenient to keep his Chamber; a Council being appointed, Mr. *Walker* and Major *Baker* meeting him there, desired him to continue his Government; and that he might be assur'd of all the assistance they could give him; but he positively refused to concern himself any further. The Commission he bore, as well as their respect for his Person, made it a duty in them to contribute all they could to his safety; and therefore, finding him desirous to escape the danger of such a Tumult, they suffered him to disguise himself, and in a Sally, for the relief of *Culmore*, to pass in a Boat with a load of Match on his back, from whence he got to the Shipping.

April

April 19. The *Garrison* seeing they were deserted, are left without a Governour, and having resolv'd to maintain the Town, and to defend it against the Enemy, they considered of some person they could have confidence in, to direct them in the management of this Affair, and unanimously resolv'd to choose Mr. *Walker*, and Major *Baker*, to be their Governours dureing the Siege; but these Gentlemen considering the importance, as well as the uncertainty of such an office, acquainted, by Letter, Col. *Cuningham*, (whose business they thought it was to take care of them) with this matter, and desired him to undertake the Charge; but he being obliged by his instructions, to obey the Orders of Collonel *Lundy*, thought fit to make other measures. They then accepted the Government of the Garrison. These Gentlemen chose Eight Collonels, and Regimented the men in this order :

    Col. *Walker* 15 Companies.

    Colonel *Baker* 25 Companies.

    Col. *Crofton* 12 Comp.

    Col. *Michelburn*, 17 Comp, formerly Col. *Skivingtons* Regiment.

    Col. *Lance* 13 Comp.

    Col. *Muntro* 13 Comp. formerly Col. *Whitneys*.

    Col. *Hamil* 14 Comp.

Col.

Col. *Murrey* 8 Comp.

In all 117 Companies, each Comp. consisting of 60 Men. In all 7020 Men, 341 Officers.

This was our complement after having form'd our selves, as above mentioned; but the Number of Men, Women and Children in the Town, was about Thirty thousand. Upon a Declaration of the Enemy to Receive and Protect all that would desert us, and return to their dwellings, Ten Thousand left us; after that many more grew weary of us, and Seven thousand died of Diseases.

The same day our Governours view the Stores, and give other necessary Orders and directions: In the mean time they observe the motion of the Enemy, and that their Guns were so placed, that they could not draw out to their usual place of exercising, therefore they divide the Outline into Eight parts; each Regiment had its own ground, and each Company knew their own Bastion. The Drummers were all enjoyned to quarter in one house, so that on the least notice they repair'd to the respective post of the Company they belong'd to; and upon all Alarms, without any parading, all officers and private men came into their own ground and places, without the least disorder or confusion.

There

There were Eighteen Clergy-men in the Town of the Communion of the Church, who in their turns, when they were not in Action, had Prayers and Sermon every day; the Seven Nonconforming Ministers were equally careful of their people, and kept them very obedient and quiet, much different from the behaviour of their Brother Mr. *Osborn*, who was a spy upon the whole North, imployed by my Lord *Tyrconnel*, and Mr. *Hewson*, who was very troublesome, and would admit none to fight for the *Protestant Religion* till they had first taken the Covenant.

After enjoyning all parties to forget their distinctions, and to joyn as one man, in de·fence of the interest of K. *William* and Q. *Mary*, and the *Protestant Religion*, against the Enemies of both; we betake ourselves, in the first place, by order, to our several Devotions, and recommend our selves, and the Cause we undertook, to the Protection and Care of the Almighty; for we might then truly say, with the Church in the *Liturgy, there is none other that fighteth for us, but only thou, O God.* It did beget some disorder amongst us, & confusion, when we look'd about us, and saw what we were doing; our Enemies all about us and our Friends running away from us; a Garrison we had compos'd of a number of poor people, frightned from their own homes,

and

and seem'd more fit to hide themselves, than
to face an Enemy ; when we consider'd we
had no Persons of any Experience in War
among us, and those very Persons that were
sent to assist us, had so little confidence in
the Place, that they no sooner saw it, but
they thought fit to leave it : that we had but
few Horse to Sally out with, and no Forage ;
no Engineers to Instruct us in our Works ;
no Fire-works, not as much as a Hand-
Granado to annoy the Enemy ; not a Gun
well mounted in the whole Town ; that we
had so many Mouths to feed, and not above
ten days Provisions for them, in the Opinion
of our former Governours ; that every day
several left us, and gave constant intelligence
to the Enemy ; that they had so many
opportunities to divide us, and so often
endeavour'd it, and to betray the Governours ; that they were so Numerous, so
Powerful and Well appointed an Army, that
in all human probability we could not think
our selves in less danger, than the *Israelites*
at the *Red Sea*.

When we considered all this, it was obvious
enough what a dangerous undertaking we
had ventur'd upon ; but the Resolution and
Courage of our people, and the necessity we
were under, and the great confidence and
dependance among us on God Almighty, that
he

he would take care of us, and preserve us,
made us overlook all those difficulties. And
God was pleased to make us the happy instruments of preserving this Place, and to
him we give the Glory, and no one need goe
about to undervalue or lessen those he was
pleas'd to choose for so great a work ; we do
allow our selves to be as unfit for it as they
can make us, and that God has only Glori-
fied himself in working so great a wonder
with his own right hand, and his holy arm get-
ting himself the Victory.

April 20. A part of the Enemy march'd
towards *Peny-burn* hill, a place about a Mile
distant from the Town *N.B.E.* on the side of
the River, there they pitch'd their Tents, &
by that means hinder'd all passage to, and
correspondence with, *Culmore.*

We sent Mr. *Bennet* out of the Garrison,
with Orders to go to *England,* and to give
account of our Resolutions to defend the
Town against the Enemy. Our men were
order'd to fire after him, that the Enemy
might think he had deserted us.

This day my Lord *Strabane* came up to our
walls, makeing us many Proposals, and offer-
ing his Kings Pardon, Protection and Favour,
if we would surrender the Town, but these
fine words had no place with the Garrison.
At that very time of his Capitulating with us,

we

we observ'd the Enemy using that opportunity
to draw their Canon to a convenient stand,
we therefore desired his Lordship to withdraw, otherwise we would make bold to fire
at his Lordship; his Lordship continued in
his Complements, till we plainly told him, we
would never deliver the Town to any but K.
William and Q. *Mary*, or their order. My
Lord having ended all his Insinuations, found
himself at last obliged to retire.

Several Trumpets were likewise sent to us
from the Enemy, but with as little success.

April 21. The Enemy placed a *Demi-
culverin*, 180 Perches distant from the Town,
E. B. N. on the other side the water: they
play'd at the houses in the Town, but did
little or no mischief only to the Market-
house.

This day our Men Sallied out, as many as
pleased, and what Officers were at leasure,
not in any commendable Order, yet they
killed above 200 of the Enemies Souldiers,
besides *Mamow* the *French* General, and
several other Officers whose Names you will
find in the annexed List. A party of Horse
came with great fury upon the Salliers, and
forced their retreat, which they made good
with the loss of four private Men, and one
Lieutenant *Mac. Phedris*, whom our Men
brought off; and having leisure and more
concern

concern *then* upon us for the loss, then afterwards on such occasions, we buried them with some Ceremony. We had at this time 50 Horse Commanded by Col. *Murry;* upon whom they press'd so hard at first, that some of his Horse were beaten to the very Gates ; so that Mr. *Walker* found it necessary to mount one of the Horses and make them rally, and to Relieve Col. *Murry,* whom he saw surrounded with the Enemy, and with great Courage laying about him. In this Action we took three pair of Colours.

April 23. The besiegers planted four *Demi-culverins* in the lower end of Mr. *Strongs* Orchard, near 80 Perches distant from the Town, opposite to *Ship-key-Street:* these playing incessantly, hurt several People in the Houses, battered the Walls and Garrets, so that none could Lodge safely above Stairs. The besieged make due returns to their Firing from the Bastions, kill'd Lieut. *Fitz Patrick*, Lieut. Col. *O Neale*, two Serjeants, and several Souldiers ; and besides these, two *Friars* in their Habits, to the great Grief of the Enemy, that the Blood of those Holy Men should be spilt by such an Heretical Rabble, as they called the besieged.

April 25. The plac'd their Mortar-pieces in the said Orchard, and from thence play'd a few small Bombs, which did little hurt to
the

the Town, all of them lighting in the Streets,
except one which kill'd an old Woman in a
Garret; from the same place they threw
afterwards many larger Bombs, the first of
which fell into a House while several Officers
were at Dinner; it fell upon the Bed of the
Room they were in, but did not touch any
of them; forced into a lower Room, and
kill'd the Landlord, and broke down one side
of the House, and made a large passage for
the Guests to come out at instead of the
Doors it had choaked up.

April 28. The besieged made another
Sally, and killed several of the Enemy at
Penyburn-Hill, but were forced to Retreat,
being pressed by the Enemies Horse, who
charged us on all sides. In this Action we
lost only two Men, had eight or ten wounded,
which in a few days recovered, and were fit
for Service.

This day by a shot from one of our Bastions, the Enemies Gunner was kill'd, and
one of his Guns broken.

May 5. This Night the Besiegers draw a
Trench cross the *Wind-Mill Hill*, from the
Bog to the River, and there begin a Battery;
from that they endeavour'd to Annoy our
Walls; but they were too strong for the
Guns they us'd, and our Men were not afraid
to advise them to save all that Labour and
Expence;

Expence ; that they always kept the Gates open, and they might use that Passage if they pleas'd, which was wider than any Breach they could make in the Walls.

May 6. The Besieged fearing that Battery might incommode that part of the Town nearest to it, consult how to put a stop to their further proceeding in that work ; Mr. *Walker* draws a Detachment out of each Company, of Ten Men, and after putting them into the best Order their Impatience could allow, he Sallies out at the head of them (with all imaginable Silence) at *Ferry-Key Gate*, at four of the Clock in the Morning. One troop of them beat the Enemies Dragoons from the Hedges, while the other possesses their Trenches The Dispute was soon over, and the Enemy, thô a very considerable Detachment, are so pressed by the forwardness of our Men, and discouraged at the sight of so many lying in their Blood, that they fled away, and left us the Ground we contended for, and some Booty, besides the Plunder of the Dead.

The Salliers in this Action kill'd Two hundred of their Men, most of which were shot through the Breast or Head ; Five Hundred were Wounded. Three Hundred of them within few days died of their Wounds, as we were informed by Messengers, and the
Prisoners

Prisoners we took afterwards. The account of the Officers kill'd, or taken Prisoners in this Action, you will find in the Bill annexed. Our side lost Three men, and had only Twenty wounded. At this time we took Five pair of Colours.

We sent a Drummer to desire the Enemy to send an Officer with 14 Men to bury their Dead, which they did perform very negligently, scarce covering their Bodies with Earth.

After this performance, the Enemies want of Courage, and our want of Horse occasion'd, that some Weeks produced but little Action except Skirmishes; in which Captain *Noble* was very active and successful; kills several of their Officers, and finds Letters about them that afforded some Intelligence, and particularly instructed us about the Surrender of *Culmore;* but upon what Conditions. and for how much Money, we could not understand.

Our Sallies many times began but with small parties; Capt. *Noble*, and sometimes other Officers, when they saw the Enemy make an approach, wou'd run out with about Ten or Twelve men at their Heels, and Skirmish'd a while with them : When the Besieged saw them Engaged, and in any danger, they issued out in greater numbers

to

to their Relief, and always came off with great Execution on the Enemy, and with very little loss to themselves.

In all these Sallies we lost none of any Note, but Lieutenant *Douglas* and Captain *Cuningham*, whom the Enemy took Prisoner, and after Quarter given, basely Murdred. They did not want being reproach'd with so signal an Instance of their Cruelty and breach of Faith, neither did they want Impudence to deny it by the addition of many bloody Oaths and Protestations ; but it was too evident by the Testimony of their own Officers and Souldiers, that were afterwards our Prisoners. But this sort of proceeding was very usual with them, and agreeable to an account we had of their obligation by Oath and Resolutions, not to keep Faith with us, and to break whatever Articles were given us : Which a Prisoner with us, (troubled in Conscience, that he had engaged himself with so wicked and perfidious Men) discover'd to us.

We were convinced of the Truth of it by some Examples they gave us after this : When they hung out a *White Flag* to invite us to a Treaty, Mr. *Walker* ventur'd out to come within hearing of my Lord *Lowth* and Colonel *O Neale*, and in his passage had an hundred Shot fired at him ; he got the
shelter

shelter of a House, and upbraiding them
with this Treachery, bid them order their
Men to be quiet or he wou'd order all the
Guns on the Walls to fire at them ; They
deny'd they knew anything of it : And this
was all the satisfaction to be expected from
persons of such a Principle.   At another
time the Enemy desired one *White* might
have leave to come to them; the Besieged
sent him in a little *Boat*, with two Men, upon
Parol, which they broke very dishonourably,
keeping both the Men and Boat with them.
The loss of the Boat was considerable to
us, for the Gentlemen that left us took all
our Boats, and left them to the Sea and Wind,
and this was the only Boat we had remaining.

The Enemy remove their Main Body from
St. *Johnstown*, and pitch their Tents upon
Belyougry-Hill, about two Miles distant from
Derry S.S.W.   They place Guards on all
sides of the Town, so that the Besieged
found it impossible to receive or convey any
Intelligence, and great difficulty to come to
the Wells for Water, which they often Fought
for, and cost some of them their Blood.   One
Gentleman had a Bottle broke at his Mouth
by a Shot ; yet the Water of the Town was
so muddy and troubled with our continual
Firing, and so many going to it, that we were
forced to run those hazards.

June

June 4. The Besiegers made an Attack at the *Wind-Mill Works*, with a Body of Foot and Horse; the Horse they divided into three Squadrons, and assaulted us at the River side, it being Low water; the Foot Attack the rest of our Line. The Front of the Horse was composed of Gentlemen that had bound themselves by an Oath, that they wou'd mount our Line; they were commanded by Captain *Butler*, second son of my Lord *Montgarret*. Our men place themselves within our Line in three Ranks, so advantageously that one Rank was always ready to march up and relieve the other, and discharge successively upon the Enemy, which (thô 'tis strange how they could think otherwise) was great surprize and astonishment to them; for they it seems expected we should make but one single Volley, and then they cou'd fall in upon us. Their Foot had Fagots laid before them for a defence against our Shot; they and the Horse began with a loud *Huzza*, which was seconded from all parts of their Camp with most dreadful shrieks and howlings of a numerous Rabble that attended the Enemy. The Fagot Men are not able to stand before our Shot, but are forced to quit their New defence and Run for it : Capt. *Butler* tops our work, which was but a dry Bank of 7 foot high at the Water side

side, and thirty of his Sworn party of Horse
follow him. Our Men wondred to find they
had spent so many Shot, and that none of
them fell : but Capt. *Crooke* observed they
had Armour on and then commanded to Fire
at their Horses, which turn'd to so good
account, that but three of these bold Men
with much difficulty made their Escape. We
wonder'd the Foot did not (according to
Custom) run faster, till we took notice that
in their Retreat they took the dead on their
backs, and so preserv'd their own Bodies
from the remainder of our Shot, which was
more Service than they did when alive.

The Enemy in this Action lost 400 of their
fighting Men, most of their Officers were
kill'd. Captain *Butler* was taken Prisoner, and
several others, which are mentioned in the
List. We lost on our side six Private Men,
and one Captain *Maxwell;* two of the Men
were kill'd by a Shot of a great Gun from the
other side the Water, opposite to the *Wind-
Mill Works.*

This Night, the Enemy from *Strong-
Orchard* play their Bombs which were 273
pound weight apiece, and contained several
pounds of Powder in the Shell ; they plowed
up our Streets, and broke down our Houses,
so that there was no passing the Streets nor
staying within Doors, but all flock to the
Walls

Walls, and the Remotest parts of the Town,
where we continued very safe, while many of
our sick were kill'd being not able to leave
their Houses: They plied the Besieged so
close with great Guns in the Day time, and
Bombs in the Night, and sometimes in the
Day, that they could not enjoy their rest,
but were hurry'd from place to place, and
tyer'd into faintness and diseases, which de-
stroy'd many of the Garison, which was
reduced to 6185 men the 15 of this Month:
these Bombs were some advantage to us, on
one account, for being under great want of
Fuel, they supply'd us plentifully from the
Houses they threw down, and the Timber
they broke for us.

June 7. Three Ships come up to *Killmore
Fort*, and fired at the Castle, and attempted
coming up the River, but one of them unfortu-
nately run aground, and lay some time at the
Mercy of the Enemies Shot, and so much on
her side, she could not make any return;
but at length with some pleasure we saw her
get off, and, as we believed, without much
loss or damage.

June 15. We discovered a Fleet of 30 Sail
of Ships in the *Lough*, which we believed
came from *England* for our Relief, but we
could not propose any method to get intelligence from them, and we did fear it was
impossible

impossible they could get to us, and the
Enemy now begin to watch us more narrowly.
They raise Batteries opposite to the Ships,
and line both sides of the River with great
numbers of Fire locks.   They draw down
their Guns to *Charles-Fort*, a place of some
strength upon the Narrow part of the River,
where the Ships were to pass; here they
contrived to place a Boom of Timber, joyned
by Iron Chains, and fortified by a Cable of
12 Inches thick Twisted round it; They made
this Boom first of Oak, but that could not
float, and was soon broke by the force of the
water : Then they made one of Firr beams
which answered their purpose better; it was
fastened at one end through the Arch of a
Bridg, at the other by a piece of Timber
forced into the ground and fortified with piece
of stone work.   This account, as we had it
from the Prisoners, did much trouble us, and
scarce left us any hopes; We made several
signs to the Ships from the Steeple, and they
to us from their Ships, but with very little
information to either.   At last a Messenger
got to us, one *Roch*, from Major-General *Kirk*
who got to the Water-side over-against us,
and then swam cross the River; he gave us
an account of the Ships, Men, Provisions and
Arms in them for our relief, the great
concern of the Major General for us, and his
care

care and desire to get with his Ships up to
the Town. He sent another Messenger along
with this, one *Crumy* a Scotch man, to give
us this account, and to know the Condition
of our Garison, but he was taken prisoner :
There was soon an understanding between
him and the Enemy, he is instructed to
frame a Message much differing from the
other ; they hang out a white Flag, inviteing
us to a parlee ; they tell us we are under
great mistakes about the Major General, and
our expectation of relief from *England*, that
they were all there in confusion, and that we
might have leave to inform ourselves further
from the Messenger they had taken, either
in private or publick : We sent some to that
purpose, but they soon discovered the cheat,
and returned to us with other particular ac-
counts of his Treachery.

We received further intelligence in *July* by
a little Boy, that with great Ingenuity made
two dispatches to us from the Major General
at *Inch*. One Letter he brought ty'd in his
Garter, another at his second coming within
a Cloth Button. We sent our first answer
made up within a piece of a Bladder, in the
shape of a Suppositor, and the same way
applied to the Boy ; Our second Answer he
carry'd within the folding of his Breeches, and
falling among the Enemy, for fear of a
discovery

discovery he swallowed the Letter, and after some short confinement and endeavour to extort some thing from him, he made his escape again to the Major General.

Major General *Kirk's* Letter to Mr. *Walker*.

Sir,

I *Have received yours by the way of* Inch : *I writ to you Sunday last, that I would endeavour all means Imaginable for your relief, and find it impossible by the River, which made me send a party to* Inch, *where I am going my self to try if I can beat off their Camp, or divert them, so that they shall not press you. I have sent Officers, Ammunition, Arms, great Guns, &c. to* Iniskillin, *who have* 3000 *Foot and* 1500 *Horse, and a Regiment of Dragoons, that has promised to come to their relief, and at the same time I will attack, the Enemy by* Inch; *I expect* 6000 *Men from* England *every Minute, they having bin Shipt these 8 days; I have Stores and Victuals for you, and am resolved to relieve you.* England *and* Scotland *are in a good posture, and all things very well setled; be good Husbands of your Victuals, and by Gods help we shall overcome these Barbarous People: Let me hear from you as often as you can, and the Messenger shall have what reward he will. I have several of the Enemy has deserted to me, who all assure me they cannot stay long: I hear from* Iniskillin *the Duke of* Barwick *is beaten, I pray God it be true, for then nothing can hinder them joyning you or me. Sir,* Your faithful Servant,

To Mr. George Walker. J. Kirke.

But to return to our Story, the Besieged send

send many a longing look towards the Ships,
their Allowance being very small, as you may
see by the Account of the Allowances out of
the Store : They build a Boat of 8 Oars a side,
and Man it well, with intent to make to the
Fleet and give the Major General an account
of the sad Condition we were in ; they set out
with the best of our Wishes and Prayers but
were forced to return, it being impossible they
could indure the Showers of Shot that were
poured in upon them from each side the River.

June 18. Captain *Noble* went up the River,
and took twenty Men along with him, with a
design to Rob the Fish-House, but was pre-
vented by Alarum from the Enemies Boats ;
however he Engaged them, killed a Lieutenant, one Ensign, and five private Men, took
fourteen Prisoners and both their Boats. The
Boats we offer'd to return, and to give the
best Prisoner we had, for leave to send a Messenger to the Ships ; but we could not prevail :
We had agreed for five Hundred pound for
L.Col. *Talbot's* Ransom, (commonly called
Wicked Will) we profer'd him his liberty, and
to remit the Mony on the same score, but we
could not obtain this favour upon any Terms :
Soon after the Lieutenant Col. died of his
Wounds, and we lost the benefit of our bar-
gain ; Tho' we took all Imaginable care to keep
him alive, permitted him his Chirurgeon and
Diet

Diet from the Enemy, at times agreed on,
Favours that we allow'd all the Prisoners,
when we were starving our selves, which we
did not put any great value on, but that the
Enemy so ill deserv'd them. At this time
Governor *Baker* is very dangerously ill, and
Col. *Michelburn* is chosen and appointed to
assist Governor *Walker*, that when one Commanded in Sallies the other might take care
of the Town ; and if one shou'd fall the Town
might not be left without a Government, and
to the hazard of new Elections.

June 24. or thereabouts, *Conrad de Rosen*,
Marshal General of the *Irish* Forces, is received into the Enemies Camp ; and finding
how little the Enemy had prevail'd against
us, expressed him self with great Fury against
us, and swore by the Belly of God, He would
demolish our Town and bury us in its Ashes,
putting all to the Sword, without consideration of Age or Sex, and wou'd study the
most exquisite Torments to lengthen the
misery and pain of all he found obstinate, or
active in opposing his Commands and Pleasure ; But these Threatnings, as well as
his Promises in which he was very eloquent
and obliging had very little power with us ;
God having under all our Difficulties establish'd us with a Spirit and Resolution above
all Fear or Temptation to any mean Com-
pliances

pliances, we having devoted our Lives to the
defence of our City, our Religion, and the
Interest of King *William* and Queen *Mary*.

For fear any one should contrive Surrendring the Town, or move it to the Garrison,
the Governour made an Order, That no such
thing should be mention'd upon pain of
Death.

Every day some or other Deserted the
Garrison, so that the Enemy receiv'd constant Intelligence of our proceedings. This
gave some trouble and made us remove our
Ammunition very often, and contrive many
other Amusements. Our *Iron Ball* is now
all spent, and instead of them we make *Balls*
of *Brick*, cast over with *Lead*, to the weight
and size of our *Iron-Ball*. The Gunners did
not pretend to be great Artists, yet they were
very industrious and scarce spent a Shot
without doing some remarkable Execution.

The *Marshal de Rosen* orders 3 Mortar
pieces and several Pieces of Ordnance against
the *Windmill* side of the Town, as also two
Culverins opposite to *Butchers-Gate;* He runs
a Line out of *Bog-street* up within ten Perches
of the half Bastion of that Gate, in order to
prepare Matters for laying and springing a
Mine; He made approaches to our Line,
designing to hinder the Relief of our Out-
guards, and to give us trouble in fetching

D   Water

Water from *Colum-kills Well*; He defends
his Line with a strong Guard in hopes to
seize our Out-works, if we shou'd chance to
be negligent in our Posts and neglect keeping good Guards. By the contrivance of
our Governour and Colonel *Michelburn*, and
the directions and care of Captain *Shomberg*,
or rather being instructed by the Working,
Motions and Example of the Enemy, as
well as we could observe them ; We Counter-
mine the Enemy before the *Butchers-Gate*,
the Governour contrives a Blind to preserve
our Work from the Enemies Battery. The
Enemy Fired continually from their Trenches,
and we make them due returns with sufficient damage to them ; for few days passed,
but some of the choice and most forward of
their Men fell by our Arms and Firing.

June 30. At ten of the clock at night my
L. *Clancarty*, at the Head of a Regiment,
and with some Detachments, possesses himself of our Line, and enters some Miners in
a low Cellar under the half Bastion. Capt.
Noble, Capt. *Dunbar* and several other
Gentlemen sally by Order at the *Bishops-
Gate*, and creep along the Wall till they
came very near the Enemies Guards ; our
Men receive their Firing quietly, til they
got to a right distance, and then thundred
upon them. Our Case-Shot from the Bastion

tion and small Shot off the Walls second the
Sallier's Firing so effectually, that his Lordship was forc'd to quit his Post, and hasten
to the main Body of the Enemy, and to
leave his Miners and an hundred of his best
Men dead upon the place ; besides, several
Officers and Souldiers were wounded, and
died of their Wounds some days after this
Action, as we were informed. We were often
told, That some great thing was to be perform'd by this Lord ; and they had a Pro-
phecy among them, *That a* Clancarty *should
knock at the Gates of* Derry ; the credulity
and superstition of his Country, with the
vanity of so brave an Attempt, and some
good Liquor, easily warm'd him to this bold
Undertaking ; But we see how little value
is to be put on *Irish* Prophesies, or Courage
so supported.

June 30. Governor *Baker* dies, his death
was a sensible loss to us, and generally
lamented, being a Valiant person ; in all his
Actions among us shew'd the greatest Honour, Courage and Conduct, and would it suit
a design of a Journal, might fill a great
share of this Account with his Character.

And indeed there were so many great
things done by all our Officers and Men, and
so often, that 'tis impossible to account them
all ; but certainly never People in the World
behaved

behaved themselves better, and they cannot want mentioning upon other occasion, where it may be more to their advantage than to fill this Paper with their Story.

About this time Lieutenant Gen. *Hamilton* offers Conditions to the Garrison, and they seem to hearken to them, till they had us'd that opportunity to search for Provision to support the great Necessity of the Garrison, which was now brought to that extremity, that they were forc'd to feed upon Horse flesh, Dogs, Cats, Rats and Mice, Greaves of a year old, Tallow, and Starch, of which they had good quantities, as also salted and dried Hides, &c. yet they unanimously resolv'd to eat the *Irish,* and then one another, rather than surrender to any but their own King *William* and Queen *Mary.* Our Answer to the Lieutenant General was, *That we much wonder'd he shou'd expect we cou'd place any confidence in him, that had so unworthily broke Faith with our king; That he was once gene-rously trusted, thô an Enemy, yet betray'd his Trust, and we cou'd not believe that he had learn'd more sincerity in an* Irish *Camp.*

General *Rosen* sends us a Letter to this effect, *That if we did not deliver the Town to him by Six of the Clock in the Afternoon on the* 1st *day of* July, *according to Lieutenant Gen.* Hamilton's *proposals, he wou'd dispatch*
his

his Orders as far as Balishanny, Charlimont, Belfast, *and the Barony of* Inishowen, *and rob all Protected, as well as Unprotected Protestants, that were either related to us, or of our Faction, and that they shou'd be driven under the Walls of* Derry, *where they should perish, if not reliev'd by the Besieged.* He threatned, *to burn and lay waste all our Country, if there should appear the least probability of any Troops coming for our Relief: Yet, if the Garrison would become Loyalists* (as they termed it) *and Surrender the Town on any tolerable Conditions, he would protect them from all Injuries and give them his Favour.* But the Besieged receive all these Proposals with contempt and some indignation, which did produce some heat and disorder in the Mareschal.

Among the Bombs thrown into the Town, there was one dead Shell, in which was a Letter declaring to the Souldiers the Proposals made by the Lieutenant General; for they imagined them Strangers to their Condescensions, and that their Officers wou'd not communicate such things to them. Copies also of these Proposals were conveyed into Town by Villains, who disperse them about the Town, but all to no purpose; for they will not entertain the least thought of Surrendring, and it would cost a mans life to speak of it, it was so much abhor'd.

July

July 2. The Enemy drive the poor Protestants, according to their threatning, under our Walls, Protected, and Unprotected, Men, Women and Children and under great distresses. Our Men at first did not understand the meaning of such a Crowd, but fearing they might be Enemies, Fired upon them; we were troubled when we found the mistake, but it supported us to a great degree, when we found that none of them were touch'd by our Shot, which by the direction of Providence (as if every Bullet had its Commission what to do) spared them, and found out and kill'd three of the Enemy, that were some of those that drove the poor People into so great a danger. There were some Thousands of them, and they did move great Compassion in us, but warm'd us with new rage and fury against the Enemy, so that in sight of their Camp we immediately erect a Gallows, and signified to them we were resolved to hang their Friends that were our Prisoners, if they did not suffer these poor People to return to their own Houses.

We send to the Enemy, that the Prisoners might have Priests to prepare them after their own Methods for death; but none came. We upbraid them with breach of Promises, and the Prisoners detect their barbarity, declaring, *They could not blame us to put them to death,*
                                                  seeing

*seeing their People exercis'd such Severity and
Cruelty upon our poor Friends, that were under
their Protections.* They desired leave from the
Governor, to write to L. G. *Hamilton;* they
had a much better opinion of him than we
cou'd be perswaded into; yet we allow a
Messenger to carry the following Letter to
him from their Prisoners.

My Lord,

U *Pon the hard dealing the Protected (as well as
other Protestants) have met withal in being
sent under the Walls, you have so incens'd the
Governor and others of this Garrison that we are
all condemn'd by a Court Martial to dye to morrow,
unless those poor People be withdrawn. We have
made application to Marshal General de* Rosen;
*but having received no Answer, we make it our
Request to you (as knowing you are a person that
does not delight in shedding innocent Blood) that
you will represent our condision to the Martial
General. The Lives of 20 Prisoners lye at stake,
and therefore require your diligence and care. We
are all willing to die (with our Swords in our hands)
for His Majesty: but to suffer like Malefactors is
hard, nor can we lay our Blood to the charge of
the Garrison, the Governor and the rest having
used and treated us with all Civility imaginable.
We remain*

Your most dutiful and dying Friends,

Netervill, Writ by another hand, he himself has
lost the Fingers of his Right hand.

To L. G. *Hamilton.* 　　*E. Butler, G. Aylmor,
—MacDonnel,—Darcy, &c.*
In the Name of all the rest.
The

The Lieutenant General, to shew his great concern for his Friends, returns this Answer to our Prisoners Letter.

Gentlemen,

*I*N *Answer to yours ; What those poor People are like to suffer, they may thank themselves for, being their own fault ; which they may prevent by accepting the Conditions have been offer'd them ; and if you suffer in this it cannot be help'd, but shall be reveng'd on many Thousands of those People (as well innocent as others) within or without that City.*

Yours *R. Hamilton.*

But however the sight of our Gallows and the Importunity of some Friends of those that were to suffer upon them, prevailed upon the Lieutenant General : So that *July* 4. the poor Protestants have leave to repair to their several Habitations ; we took down the Gallows, and order'd the Prisoners to their usual Apartments. Our Garrison now consisted of 5709 Men, and to lessen our number yet more, we crowded 500 of our useless People among the Protestants under the Walls, who pass'd undiscover'd with them, thô the Enemy suspected the design ; and to distinguish them, they pretended of finding them out by the smell. We also got into our Garrison some Effectual Men out of their number : They were in a most miserable condition, yet

dreaded

dreaded nothing more than our pity of them,
and willingness to receive them ; begging of
us on their knees, not to take them into the
Town, but chose rather to perish under our
Walls, than to hazard us within them.

The Governour has several Intimations given
him by a Friend in the Enemies Camp, That
he should look to himself, that some mischief
was intended him.   Soon after this he under-
stood some Jealously was entertain'd among
the Souldiers, That he had great quantity of
Provisions hid in his House.   Some of the
Garrison improv'd this to that degree, that
there was great danger of a Mutiny among the
Men, and that he then began to remember the
Caution was given ; but by his Instructions
to a Souldier, that was to pretend, he himself
had the same Suspicion ; it was contriv'd that
the House was privately search'd, and their
Curiosity being satisfied, they return to the
good Opinion of their Governour.

He observ'd likewise, that the Enemy had
endeavour'd to insinuate to the Garrison,
That he was to betray the Town to King
James, and was to be highly prefer'd for the
Service.   This put them in mind of a Message that one Mr. *Cole* brought to Mr. *Walker*
in the beginning of *May* last, and however
it was then supprest, the Story is now reviv'd,
and the Governour in some danger ——Mr.
Cole

Cole being taken by the Enemy, and continuing their Prisoner for some time, is at last admitted to some discourse with the Lieutenant General, who enquired particularly, what sort of person Mr. *Walker* was ; who he was most intimate with ? Mr. *Cole* (among several of Mr. *Walker's* Friends) at last names himself, hoping by this means to be employ'd on a Message to him and to obtain his liberty. The Lieutenant General ask'd, *Whether he wou'd do Service for K.* James, *and carry some Proposals he had orders to make to Mr.* Walker ? He told he wou'd ; and upon this immediately he had a Pass given him, and is dispatch'd upon a Message to Mr. *Walker.* Mr. *Cole* being got safe into the Town, was receiv'd with great Joy, and so well pleas'd with his liberty that he forgot his Business, only casually mentions it to some of the Garrison, with other discourse. Mr. *Walker* (after this) meeting several of them, they Saluted him by some great Names and Titles.

Mr. *Walker* easily saw the danger of this, and finding it was occasion'd by Discourses of Mr. *Cole*, he order'd him immediately to be confin'd ; and being examin'd he unriddles the Mystery, and gave all People satisfaction, so that they remain'd in no more doubt of their Governour.

But under these, and many other such like
circumstances

circumstances, the Governour (not without some trouble and industry) reassum'd his Credit with the Garrison, which God was pleased to preserve to him in spight of all the inventiós and designs to the contrary.

From our Works we cou'd talk with the Enemy ; several of our Men gave account of Discourses with the *Irish*, *That they express'd great prejudice and hatred of the* French, *Cursing those Damn'd Fellows that walked in Trunks* (meaning their *Jack-Boots*) *that had all Preferments in the Army that fell, and took the Bread out of their Mouths, and they believ'd wou'd have all the Kingdom to themselves at last.*

July 8. The Garrison now is reduced to 5520
July 13. The Garrison reduced to—— 5313
July 17. The Garrison is reduced to— 5114
July 22. The Garrison reduced to—— 4973
July 25. The Garrison reduced to—— 4892

This Day the Besieged made another Sally, which was performed after this manner : The day before we had a Council of War and all sworn to Secresie ; the result of which was, That the next day at Three in the morning, 200 Men should Sally out of *Bishops Gate*, 200 Men at *Butchers Gate*, and 1100 should be ready within the Ravelin for a Reserve. Our design was to bring in some of the Enemies Cattle ; they surprized the Enemy
in

(60)

in their Trenches. One Regiment draws up against them in good Order, but had only three of their Matches lighted; we came upon them over against *Butchers-Gate* and kill'd 300 of their Men, besides Officers. The Execution had been much greater, but many of our Men being much weakened with Hunger were not able to pursue them, some falling with their own blows. We return'd without any purchase of Cattle, but were advis'd to a more easie Experiment; having one Cow left, we ty'd her to a Stake, and set Fire to her. We had hopes given us, that by the Cry and Noise she wou'd make, the Enemies Cattle would be disturbed and come to her relief; and they began to move and set up their Tails, so that we hoped to have gain'd our point; but the Cow got loose, and turn'd to no account, only the danger of losing her.

July 27. The Garrison is reduced to 4456 Men, and under the greatest extremity for want of Provision, which does appear by this Account taken by a Gentleman in the Garrison, of the price of our Food.

	l.	s.	d.	
Horse flesh sold for	0	1	8	*per* pound.
A Quarter of a Dog	0	5	6	fatned by eat-
A Dogs Head	0	2	6	ing the Bodies
A Cat	0	4	6	of the slain
A Rat	0	1	0	*Irish.*
A Mouse	0	0	6	

A

A small Flook taken in the River, not to be bought for Mony, or purchased under the rate of a quantity of Meal.

A pound of Greaves— 0—1—0
A pound of Tallow — 0—4—0
A pound of salted Hides —1—0
A quart of Horse blood 0—1—0
A Horse-pudding ———0—0—6
An handful of Sea wreck—0—2
            of Chick-weed 0—1
A quart of Meal when found, 1—0

We were under so great Necessity, that we had nothing left unless we could prey upon one another: A certain Fat Gentleman conceived himself in the greatest danger, and fancying several of the Garrison lookt on him with a greedy Eye, thought fit to hide himself for three days. Our drink was nothing but Water, which we paid very dear for, and cou'd not get without great danger; We mixt in it Ginger and Anniseeds, of which we had great plenty; Our necessity of Eating the Composition of Tallow and Starch, did not only Nourish and Support us, but was an Infallible Cure of the Looseness; and recovered a great many that were strangely reduced by that Distemper, and preserved others from it.†

The Governour being with good Reason apprehensive, that these Discouragements might at length

† Note, That in the midst of this Extremity, the Spirit and Cou-

overcome

overcome that Resolution the Garrison had so long continued, considers of all imaginable methods to support them, and finding in himself still that confidence, That God would not (after so long and miraculous a Preservation) suffer them to be a prey to their Enemies, Preaches in the Cathedral, and encourages their Constancy, and endeavours to establish them in it, by reminding them of several Instances of Providence given them since they first came into that place, and of what consideration it was to the Protestant Religion at this time ; and that they need not doubt, but that God would at last deliver them from the Difficulties they were under.

rage of the Men was so great, that they were often heard discourse confidently and with some Anger contend Whether they should take their *Debentures in Ireland* or in *France*, when alas ! they cou'd not promise themselves 12 hours Life.

July 30. About an hour after Sermon being in the midst of our Extremity, we saw some Ships in the *Lough* make towards us, and we soon discovered they were the Ships Major General *Kirk* had sent us, according to his promise, When we could hold out no longer, that he would be sure to relieve us, to the hazard of himself, his Men and his Ships.

The *Mountjoy* of *Derry*, Captain *Browning* Commander, the *Phœnix* of *Colrain*, Captain *Douglas*

Douglas Master; Being both Loaden with Provision, were Convoy'd by the *Dartmouth-Frigat.* The Enemy Fired most desperately upon them from the Fort of *Culmore,* and both Sides the River; and they made sufficient returns, and with the greatest bravery. The *Mountjoy* made a little stop at the Boom, occasioned by her Rebound after striking and breaking it, so that she was run a-ground; Upon this the Enemy set up the loudest *Huzza's,* and the most dreadful to the besieged that ever we heard: Fired all their Guns upon her, and were preparing their Boats to Board her; Our trouble is not to be expressed at this dismal Prospect, but by great Providence firing a Broad side, the shock loosned her so that she got clear, and passed their Boom. Captain *Douglas* all this while was Engaged, and the *Dartmouth* gave them very warm Entertainment: At length the Ships got to us, to the unexpressible Joy and Transport of our distressed Garrison, for we only reckon'd upon two days Life, and had only nine lean Horses left, and among us all one Pint of Meal to each Man; Hunger and the Fatigue of War had so prevail'd among us, that of 7500 Men Regimented, we had now alive but about 4300, whereof at least one fourth part were rendered unserviceable.

The Besieged had only 800 men slain by the Enemy.

This

This brave Undertaking added to the great Success God had blessed us with in all our Attempts, so discourag'd the Enemy, that on the last of *July*, they ran away in the Night time, rob'd and burnt all before them for several Miles, leaving nothing with the Country People, but what they hid the Night before, in which their Care was so great, that Provision grew very plentiful after it.

In the next Morning our Men, after refreshment with a proper share of our new Provisions, went out to see what was become of the Enemy; they saw them on their March, and pursued them a little too far, so that the Rear-Guard of the Enemies Horse turned upon them, and killed seven of our Men.

They encamped at *Strabane*, but hearing of the Defeat of their Forces under L. General *Maccarty*, by the *Inniskilling* Men, they removed their Camp, and thought fit to make some haste to get farther off; they broke into pieces four of their great Guns, and threw twelve Cartloads of Arms and Ammunition into the River.

The besieged took above 2000 Arms from the Enemy, besides Money and Clothes, &c.

Thus after 105 days, being close besieged by near 20000 Men constantly supplied from *Dublin*, God Almighty was pleased in our greatest

greatest Extremity to send Relief, to the Admiration and Joy of all good People, and to the great dissappointment of so powerful and inveterate an Enemy ; who were concerned in point of Interest, as well as Reputation to have Rendered themselves Masters of that Town.

The Enemy lost between eight or nine thousand Men before our Walls, and a hundred of their best Officers, according to the best Computation we could make of both, by the Information of the Prisoners we took, most of these fell by the Sword, the Rest of Fevers and Flux ; and the *French* Pox, which was very remarkable on the Bodies of several of their dead Officers and Soldiers.

We are now under some Impatience to see Major-General *Kirk*, under God and the King, our Deliverer.

Aug. 1. The Governor orders C. *White*, C. *Dobbin*, C. J. *Hamilton*, Capt. *Jenny*, and Mr. *Jo. Fox*, both Clergy-men, to wait on the Major-General at *Inch*, to give him an account of the raising the Siege, and to carry him our Thanks, and desire him to come and receive the Garrison. The next day the Major-General sent to us Col. *Steward*, and Col. *Richards* the Engineer, to Congratulate our Deliverance. On *Sunday* the Major-General came into the Town, and was received by the Governor, and the whole

Garrison,

Garrison, with the greatest Joy and Acclamations. The Governor presents him with the Keys, but he wou'd not receive them. The next day the Governor (with several of his Officers) Dined with the Major-General at *Inch*; he complemented the Major-General with his Regiment, That after doing the King all the service in his power, he might return to his own Profession : But the Major-General desired him to dispose of it as he pleased, and accordingly he gave it to Captain *White*, as a mark of his Respect, and the Gentleman's known merit.

Upon this, we call a Council at *Derry*, the Governor is prevailed on to go to the King, and to carry an Address from the Garrison. The Garrison is now form'd, and of eight Regiments made into six. After assurance from the Major-General, of his Care and Favor to his Men, and particularly to his own Regiment, he took leave of them and embarked for *England*.

To the Most Excellent Majesty of WILLIAM *and* MARY, *King and Queen of* England Scotland, France, and Ireland, *Defenders of the Faith, &c.*

The humble A D D R E S S of the Governors Officers, Clergy, and other Gentlemen, in the City and Garrison of LONDONDERRY.

We

WE the most Dutiful and Loyal Subscribers of this Address, (out of a deep sense of our late miserable Estate and Condition) do hereby return our due acknowledgments to Almighty God, and to Your Sacred Majesty, and under you, to the indefatigable Care of Major-General Kirk, for our unexpected Relief by Sea, in spite of all the opposition of our industrious, but bloody and implacable Enemies; which Relief was no less wonderfully, than seasonably, conveyed to us, and that, at the very nick of time, when we (who survived many thousands that died here of Famine during the Siege) were just ready to be cut off, and perish, by the hands of barbarous, cruel, and inhuman Wretches; who no sooner saw us delivered, and that they could not compass their Wicked Designs against this Your Majesties City, and our Lives (for which they thirsted) immediately set all the Country round us on fire, after having plundered, robbed, and stripped all the Protestants therein, as well those Persons they themselves granted Protections to, as others: We do therefore most sincerely rejocie with all our Souls, and bless God for all his singular and Repeated Mercies and Deliverances: and do for ever Adore the Divine Providence for Your Majesties rightful and peaceable accession to the Imperial Crown of these Kingdoms (the proclaiming of which was justly celebrated in these Parts with Universal Joy;) and we do with all humble Submission present to Your Sacred Majesty our unfeigned Loyalty, the most valuable Tribute we can give, or your Majesty receive from us. And since the same Providence has (through much difficulty) made us so happy as to be Your Subjects, we come in the like humility

to

to lay our selves intirely at Your Royal Feet, and do most heartily and resolvedly offer and engage our Lives and Fortunes to Your Service. And further we do most unanimously join in a firm and unchangeable Vow and Resolution of improving all occasions of becoming Serviceable to Your Majesty, in what Station soever it shall please God and your Majesty to place us ; and will expose our selves to all Hazards and Extremities to serve Your Majesty against the Common Enemy. From all which Promises, Vows and Services, we and every of us promise (without any Exception or Reserve) not to recede unto our Lives end. In testimony of all which, we have hereunto subscribed our Names at Londonderry *this* 29th *day of* July, *Anno Dom.* 1689.

GEORGE WALKER
John Michelbourn
Richard Crofton
Thomas Lane
Hugh Hamill
Charles Kinaston
William Campbell
Gervase Squire
Henry Monry
Henry Campsie
Adam Morrow
John Dobbin
Alexander Steward
Thomas Gughtredge
Thomas Johnston
Thomas Newcomen
Patt Moore
John Humes

Edward Davyes
John Hamilton
Thomas Ash
Robert Boyd
Ralph Fullerton
Michael Cunningham
Joseph Johnston
Robert Bayley
William Grove
John Mc Clelland
James Graham
William Thompson
James Young
Richard Cormach
Oliver Apton
Alex. Knox
Ja. Gledstanes
John Maghlin

Robert

Robert Dennison
Marmaduke Stewart
James Fleming
Andrew Grigson
Christopher Jenny
Thomas Smyth
Bartholomew Black
John Campbell
Robert Morgan
Michael Clenaghan
Richard Fane
Stephen Godfrey
William Hamilton
Robert Rogers
Jame Galtworth
Richard Islen
Arthur Hamilton
Michael Rullack
James Stiles
James Cunningham
Archibald Mc. Culloch
Francis Obre
Alexander Sanderson
Archibald Sanderson
Arthur Noble
Philip Dunbarr
George White
Thomas White
John Logan
Alexander Rankin
Edmund Rice
Robert Walker
James Mc. Carmick
John Cochran
James Mc. Cartny

James Tracy
John Halshton
Joseph Gordon
James Hairs
Andrew Hamilton
Adam Ardock
Robert Wallace
George Church
Richard Flemin
Henry Cust
John Crofton
Benjamin Wilkins
Thomas Lane
James Blair
Dudley Phillips
John Buchanan
Edward Curling
William Church
Dalway Clements
Albert Hall
Matthew Cocken
Thomas Brunett
William Stewart
Franc. Wilson
Matt. Mc. Clellany
George Crofton
William Babington
Robert King
Adam Downing
Abraham Hilhouse
John Mucholland
Robert Bennet
William Dobbin
George Garnet
James Barrington
Warren

Warren Godfrey
John Cunningham
Henry Lane
George Walker
      Hannson
Andrew Bailly
Daniel Mons. Cuistion
John Bailly
Robert Lyndsie
Francis Boyd
James Carr
William Montgomery
James Moore
Nicholas White
John Fuller
Thomas Key
Frederick Kye
Thomas Baker
John Hering
James Hufton

Henry Pearse
Alexander Ratliffe
Thomas Odayre
John Hamilton
Henry —verett
Daniel Fisher
John Cross
William Cross
Bernard Mulhollan
David Mulhollan
Thomas Conlay
Robert Skinner
Richard Robinson
Robert Maghlin
Matthew Clarke
John Clements
William Manson
Theophilus Manson
James Manson

The DECLARATION of the Gentlemen of *Derry*, upon the News of a General Massacre intended of the Protestants, *Decemb.* 9.

TO all Christian People to whom these Presents shall come, the Mayor, Sheriffs, and Citizens of the City of Londonderry, send greeting. Having received intimation from several creditable Persons, that an Insurrection of the *Irish Papists* was intended, and by them a general Massacre of the Protestants in this Kingdom, and the same to be acted and
                    perpetrated

perpetrated on or about the 9th of this instant *December;* and being confirmed in our fear and jealousie of so horrible a Design by many palpable Insinuations, dubious Expressions, monitory Letters, and positive Informations, all conducing and concurring to beget in us a trembling Expectation of a sudden and inevitable Ruin and Destruction ; we disposed our selves to a patient and quiet resignation to the divine Providence, hoping for some deliverance and diversion of this impending Misery, or to receive from the hands of GOD such a measure of Constancy and Courage as might inable us to possess our Souls in patience, and submissively to wait the issue of so severe a Trial : Accordingly, when on the 5th. Instant part of the Earl of *Antrim's* Forces advanced to take possession of this Place, though we looked on our selves as Sheep appointed for slaughter, and on them as the Executioners of Vengeance on us, yet we contrived no other means of escape than by flight, and with all precipitation to hurry away our Families into other Places and Countries. But it pleased GOD, who watches over us, so to order things, that when they were ready to enter the City, a great number of the younger, and some of the meaner sort of the Inhabitants, run happily to the Gates and shut them, loudly denying entrance to such Guests, and obstinately refusing Obedience to us. At first we were amazed at the Enterprise, and apprehensive of the many ill Circumstances and Consequences, that might result from so rash an Undertaking; but since that, having received repeated Advertisements of the general Design,
and

and particular Informations, which may rationally induce us to believe it; and being credibly assured, that under the pretence of six Companies to quarter amongst us, a vast Swarm of *Highland* and *Irish Papists*, were on the Ways and Roads approaching to us; That some of the Popish Clergy in our Neighbour-hood, had bought up Arms, and provided an unusual Furniture of Iron Chains for Bridles, (whereof sixty were bespoke in one place) and some of them seized, and now in our Custody; We began to consider it as an especial Instance of God's Mercy towards us, that we were not delivered over as a Prey unto them, and that it pleased him to stir up the Spirits of the People so unexpectedly to provide for their and our common Safety, and Preservation: Wherefore we do declare and remonstrate to the World, that as we have resolved to stand upon our Guards, and defend our Walls; and not to admit of any Papist whatsoever to quarter amongst us, so we have firmly and sincerely determined to persevere in our Duty and Loyalty to our Sovereign Lord the King, without the least breach of Mutiny, or Seditious Opposition to his Royal Commands. And since no other Motives have prompt us to this Resolution, but to the preservation of our Lives, and to prevent the Plots and Machinations of the enemies of the *Protestant Religion;* We are encouraged to hope that the Government will vouchsafe a candid and favourable Interpretation of our Proceedings, and that all his Majesties *Protestant* Subjects will interpose with their Prayers to God, their Sollicitations to the King, and their Advice and
Assistance

Assistance to us on this so extraordinary and
immergent an Occasion, which not only have
an Influence on the rest of the Kingdom, but
may have a probable aspect towards the Interest
of the *Protestant Religion*, and may deserve a
favourable regard from all the Professors thereof in his Majesties Dominions. *GOD save the
King.*

An ORDER *of the Council of War before
the Defeat at* Claudyford.

LONDONDERRY, *April* 31. 1689.

AT a General Council of War then held,
it was resolved unanimously, that on
Munday Morning then next following, at
Ten of the Clock, all Officers and Soldiers
of Horse, Dragoons and Foot, and all other
armed men whatsoever of our Forces and
Friends, inlisted and not inlisted, that can
and will fight for their Country and Religion,
against Popery, shall appear in the fittest
ground near *Claudyford*, *Lifford*, and *Long-
Kawsy*, as shall be nearest to their several
and respective Quarters, there to draw up in
Battalions to be ready to fight the Enemy,
and preserve our Lives, and all that is dear
to us, from them ; And all Officers and
Soldiers of Horse and Foot, and Dragoons,
and others that are arm'd, are requir'd to be
then

then and there in order to the purpose aforesaid, and to bring a week's Provision at
least with them for Men, and as much Forage as they can for Horses.

Proposals made to Collonel Lundee, *Governour
of* Derry, *by Major* Stroud. *April* 13, *as
aforesaid.*

I. THE said Major proposed to the said
Governor, to defend the Castle of
Raphoe, or demolish it.

II. How inconsiderable every Troop and
Company were, that went by the names of
Troops and Companies, instancing the Regiment of my Lord *Mount-Allexander*, all then
dispersed except his own Troop, and Capt.
Upton's Troop; which both joined would
not make one good Troop.

III. That the said Major proposed to the
said Governor, that Harrows should be
thrown into the Fords, and for want thereof,
the Instruments called Round-head, which
would have answered the same purpose; and
fearing that the Proposals aforesaid might be
neglected that Night, the said Major *Strowl*
writ also to the same effect and purpose to
the Governor by Captain *Whaley*, who
delivered the same Letter accordingly; and
if these Propositions had been observed, the
Enemy could not have passed the Ford: But
not

not being observed, and on *Monday* following, finding the Enemy in good posture on
the other side of the Water, drawing Battalions down to the Ford, he drew up what
men he could to make Opposition, who cried
out, that they wanted Powder, and most of
them Arms ; and in like manner the Major
applying to the Fort near *Claudy Bridge.*
they also cried out for want of Powder ; and
from thence returning to the Horse, he found
them breaking, and after retreating near a
Mile, prevailed with them to Rally, in order
to bring off the Foot, especially the Regiment
of *Antrim*'s, which was accordingly done. At
the same time the Souldiers told me, that the
Governor was gone by, and some others,
which made him very earnest to be gone ;
saying, I would keep them there to be cut off.

Declaration of UNION, March 21. 1688.

WHereas, either by Folly, or Weakness
of Friends, or Craft and Stratagem of
Enemies, some Rumours and Reflections are
spread abroad among the Vulgar, That the
Right Honourable the Lord *Blaney*, Sir
Arthur Rawdon, Lieutenant-Colonel *Maxwel*,
and other Gentlemen and Officers of Quality,
are resolved to take Protections from the *Irish*,
and desert the General Service for Defence of
the Protestant Party in this Kingdom, to the
great

great Discouragement of such who are so
weak, as to give Credit to so False, Scan-
dalous, and Malicious a Report. For wiping
off which Aspersion, and clearing the Minds
of all Protestant Friends wheresoever, from
all Suspicions and Jealousies of that kind or
otherwise, It is hereby unanimously Declared,
Protested, and Published to all Men, by Col
Robert Lundy, Governour of *Derry*, the said
Lord *Blaney*, Sir *Arthur Rawdon*, and other
Officers and Gentlemen, subscribing hereunto, That they and their Forces and
Souldiers are entirely united among themselves, and fully, and absolutely resolved to
oppose the *Irish* Enemy with their utmost
Force, and to continue the War against them
to the last, for their own and all Protestants
Preservation in this Kingdom. And the
Committee of *London-Derry*, for themselves,
and for all the Citizens of the said City, do
hereby Declare. Protest, and Publish to all
Men, that they are heartily and sincerely
united with the said Col. *Robert Lundy*, Lord
Blaney, Sir *Arthur Rawdon*, and all others
that joyn in this Common Cause, and with
all their Force and utmost Power will labour
to carry on the said War. And if it should
happen that our Party should be so Oppress'd
by the *Irish* Enemy, that they should be
forced to retire into this City for shelter
against

against them, (which God forbid) the said Lord *Blaney*, Sir *Arthur Rawdon*, and their Forces, and all other Protestant Friends, shall be readily received into this City, and as much as in us lies, be cherished and supported by us. Dated at *London-Derry* the 21*st* of *March*, 1688.

Robert Lundy.	Alexander Lecky.
Blaney.	Francis Nevill.
William Stewart.	James Lennox.
Arthur Rawdon.	Frederick Cowsingham.
George Maxwell.	John Leslie.
James Curry.	Henry Long.
John Forward.	William Crookshanks.
Hugh Mac Gill.	Massareene.
William Ponsonby.	Clot. Sheffington.
H. Baker.	Arthur Upton.
Chich. Fortescus.	Samuel Morrison.
James Brabazon.	Thomas Cole.
John Hill.	Francis Forster.
Samuel Norman.	Ed. Cary.
Alexander Tomkins.	John Cowan.
Matt. Cocken.	Kilner Brasier.
Horas Kennedy ⎫ Sheriffs.	James Hamilton.
Edward Brookes ⎭	John Sinclare.

From on Board the Swallow, *near* Red-Castle, *at Two Afternoon, the* 15*th. of April*, 1689.

SIR,

HEaring you have taken the Field, in Order to Fight the Enemy, I have thought it necessary for His Majesty's Service,

to

to let you know there are two well-disciplined
Regiments here on Board, that may joyn you
in two days at farthest, I am sure they will
be of great Use in any Occasion, but especially for the Encouragement of Raw Men,
as I judge most of yours are : Therefore it is
my Opinion, that you only stop the Passage of
the Enemy at the Foords of *Finn*, till I can
joyn you, and afterwards, if giving Battel be
necessary, you will be in a much better posture for it than before. I must ask your
Pardon if I am too free in my Advice ;
according to the Remote Prospect I have
of things, this seems most Reasonable to
me ; but as His Majesty has left the whole
Direction of Matters to you, so you shall find
that no Man living shall more chearfully
Obey you, than

> *Your Most Humble Servant,*
> JOHN CUNNINGHAM.

---

*Orders and Instructions for our Trusty and
well-beloved,* John Cunningham
Esquire, Colonel of One of Our Vid. p. 23.
*Regiments of Foot, and upon his Death or
Absence, to* Col. Solomon Richards, *or to
the Officer in Chief, with the Regiments
whereof they are Colonels.*

> *WILLIAM.*

WILLIAM, R.

Y OU are without delay to repair to the Quarters of the Regiment under your Command, and take care that it be in a readiness to March to *Liverpool* at such a time as you shall Appoint.

Whereupon you are to go to *Liverpool,* and to Enquire what Ships there are in that Port appointed to carry over the two Regiments, whereof you and *Solomon Richards* are Colonels, to the Town of *London-Derry*; and whether the Frigat, ordered for their Convoy, be arrived there; and as soon as the said Ships and Frigat shall be in a readiness to-sail, and fitted with all Provisions necessary for the sustenance of the said Regiments in their Passage to the said Town, and for their return from thence, if there be occasion. You are to cause Col. *Richards* Regiment to go on Board, and at the same time to Order the Regiment whereof you are Colonel, to March to *Liverpool,* and to Embarque with all speed.

And whereas We have Ordered one thousand Arms to be carried to *Liverpool,* you are to cause such a number of the said Arms as shall be wanting in the said Regiments to he delivered unto them, and the residue of the said Arms and Stores now there to be put on Shipboard, and carried to *Londonderry,* to be there employed for Our Service, as the Governour of the said Town and you shall think fit.

And We having also directed the Sum of Two thousand pounds *sterling,* to be paid unto you at *Chester,* by *Matthew Anderton* Esq; Collector of
Our

Our Customs there, you are hereby Authorised
and required to receive the same, and to dispose
of the said Sum towards the necessary subsistance of the said Regiments, and for the defence
of the place, in repairing and providing what
shall be defective therein, and to such other uses
as you with the Governour shall of the said City,
with whom you are to entertain a good Correspondence and Friendship as you shall find
necessary for Our Service ; of all which Expences
you are to give Us an account by the first opportunity.

When the Particulars necessary for the
Voyage shall be fully complied with, you are
then, Wind and Weather permitting, with the
Regiments under your Command, to make the
best of your way to *Londonderry*, and being
arrived there, or near that place, you are to
make enquiry, whether the said City be yet in
the hands of the Protestants ? and whether you
may with safety put our said Regiments into the
same ? and in that case you are immediately to
acquaint Lieutenant Colonel *Robert Lundy* Our
Governour thereof, or the Commander in chief
for the time being, with Our care in sending
those Regiments and Stores ; and for the further
relief of our Protestant Subjects in those parts,
and delivering him Our Letters and Orders to
him directed, you are to Land the said Regiments and Stores, and to take care that they be
well Quartered and disposed of in the said City,
following such Directions as you shall receive
during your stay there from our said Governour
Lieutenant Colonel *Robert Lund*y, in all things
relating to Our Service.

You

You are to assure the Governour and Inhabitants of *Londonderry*, of further and greater Succours of Men, Arms, Money, and Provisions of War coming speedily from *England* for their relief, and the security of those parts, and in the mean time you are to make the best defence you can against all persons that shall attempt to besiege the said City, or to annoy our Protestant Subjects within the same.

You are to give Us an account soon after you Arrival (and so from time to time) of the condition of the place, the Fortifications, number, quality, and affection of the People, Soldiers and others therein, or in the Country thereabouts, and what quantity of Provisions of all sorts for Horse and Foot, and Dragoons, shall or may be bought up or secur'd in those parts for Our Service, without the necessity of bringing any from *England*, upon sending more Forces thither.

You are to inform Us whether Captain *James Hamilton* be arrived at *Londonderry*, and how he has disposed of the Money and Stores committed to his Charge, and in general you are to return Us an account of every thing which you in your discretion shall think requisite for Our Service.

In case you shall find it unsafe to Land the said Regiments at or near *Londonderry*, so as to put them into the Town, which you are to endeavour by all reasonable and prudent means, you are not to expose them to extraordinary hazard in so doing, but to take care that they be carried in the said Ships, and under the same Convoy, with the same Armes, Stores, Money and Provisions

visions above mentioned, to *Carrickfergus* and to endeavour the Landing of them there, if the same may be done with safety, or otherwise to *Strangford* at both or either of which places you are to use the same caution, and to follow as near as may be the like directions, as are now given you in relation to *Londonderry*, but in case you do not find it for Our Service to Land the said Regiments at any of the said Places, you are then to take care that they be brought back to the Port of *Liverpool*, giving us speedy notice for Our further Orders.   Given at Our Court at *Whitehall* the Twelfth of *March* 168⅞, in the first year of our Reign.

> *By His Majesties Command*
>
> *S H R E W S B U R Y.*

Mr. Osburn's *Letter to Sir* Arthur Royden.

Hilsburgh, March 9th, 168⅞

S I R,

ON the 6*th,* Instant I was Intro- Vid. *p.* 24. duced by my Lord *Granard* into my Lord Deputies Presence, in the Castle of *Dublin,* and have his Pass to come and go to, through and back from *Ulster,* and though I have not his Excellencies direct Commission, yet I assure your Honour, I am at least permitted by the Lord Deputy to acquaint the Chief and others of those of the *Ulster* Association

ciation with his Discourse to me, which was
to the effect following, to wit,

That his Excellency,

1. Doth not delight in blood and devasta-
tion of the said Province, but however highly
resents their taking and continuing in Arms,
and the affronts done by them to his Majesties Government thereby, and by some
Indignities done to the late Proclamation of
Clemency, issued and dated the   day
of

2. Notwithstanding whereof is willing to
receive the said Province into protection,
provided they immediately deliver up to his
Army for his Majesties use their Arms and
serviceable Horses, and provided they deliver
up to his Excellency these three Persons, to
wit,   if they
remain in this Kingdom, and can be had.

3. And for further manifestation of his
design to prevent blood, is willing to grant
safe Conduct even to the said three Persons,
or any other of their party to and from
his Excellency, or to and from Lieutenant
General *Hamilton*, Commander of a part of
his Army hereafter mentioned, if they intend
any peaceable and reasonable Treaty; but
withal, will not upon the said or any other
account stop the March of the said part of
his Army, no not for one hour; and if it
shall

shall appear in such Treaty, that they took
up Arms meerly for self-preservation, then
he will pardon even the said three Persons
also, but is hopeless that any such thing can
be made appear, seeing many of them have
already received and accepted of Commissions
from the Prince of *Orange*, and display his
Colours in the field, as his Excellency is
credibly informed.

4. If these terms be not immediately
agreed unto, he will with a part of his Army
fight them, which part he intends shall be
at *Newry* on Monday the 11*th*. Instant, which
will from thence march to *Belfast*, and from
thence to *Colerain* and *Londonderry*, as his
Excellency intends. And that the Country
Irish (not of the Army) Men, Women and
Boys, now all armed with Half-pikes and
Baggonets, in the Counties of *Cavan*, *Monaghan*, *Tyrone*, *Londonderry*, &c. will upon the
approach of the said part of the Army, and
Resistance thereunto made, immediately enter
upon a Massacree of the *British* in the said
Counties; which force and violence of the
Rabble, his Excellency says, he cannot
restrain.

These are the heads of what I can offer to
you to the best of my memory from his
Excellencies own mouth, but I intend to stay
here this night, where if you think fit, I shall
fully

fully Discourse with you of all the above Particulars, whereof I hope you will give immediate notice to all chiefly concerned in your Neighbourhood. This in haste is all from

> *S I R*,
>> Your most humble Servant,
>>> *Alexander Osborn.*

Conrad de Rosen, *Marshal General of all His Majesties Forces.*

DEclares by these presents, to the Vide Page 52. Commanders, Officers, Soldiers, and Inhabitants of the City of *London-Derry*, that in case they do not betwixt this and *Munday* next, at Six of the Clock in the Afternoon, being the first of *July* in the Year of our Lord 1689. agree to surrender the said place of *London-Derry* unto the King upon such Conditions as may be granted them according to the Instructions and Power Lieutenant General *Hamilton* formerly received from the King; that he will forthwith issue out his Orders from the Barony of *Innishowen,* and the Sea-costs round about, as far as *Charlemont*, for the gathering together of those of their Faction, whether protected or not, and cause them immediately to be brought to the Walls of *London-Derry*, where it shall be lawful for those that are in the Town (in case they have any pity of them) to open the Gates and receive them into the Town, otherwise they will be forced

forced to see their Friends and nearest Relations
all starved for want of Food, he having resolved
not to leave one of them at home, nor anything
to maintain them : And that all hopes of Succor
may be taken away, by the Landing of any
Troops in these Parts from *England*, he further
declares, That in case they refuse to submit, he
will forthwith cause all the said Country to be
immediately destroyed, that if any Succors
should be hereafter sent them from *England*,
they may perish with them for want of Food ;
besides which he has a very considerable Army,
as well for the opposing of them in all places,
that shall be judged necessary, as for the protection of all the rest of His Majesties dutiful Subjects, whose Goods and Chattles he promises to
secure, destroying all the rest that cannot be
conveniently brought into such places as he shall
judge necessary to be preserved ; and burning
the Houses and Mills, not only of those that are
in actual Rebellion, but also of their Friends and
Adherents, that no hopes of escaping may be left
for any Man ; beginning this very day to send
his necessary Orders to all Governors and other
Commanders of His Majesties Forces, at *Colerain,
Antrim, Carrigfergus, Belfast, Dunganon, Charlemont, Belturbat, Sligo*, to Colonel *Sarsefield* Commanding a flying Army beyond *Ballishany*, Col.
Sutherland Commanding another towards *Innis-
kellin*, and the Duke of *Berwick* another on *Fyn-
wather*, to cause all the Men, Women, and Children, who are any ways Related to those in
London-Derry, or anywhere else in open Rebellion, to be forthwith brought to this place, without hopes of withdrawing further into the
Kingdom

Kingdom; that in case before the said *Munday*, the first of *July* in the Year of our Lord 1689, be expired, they do not send us Hostages, and other Deputies, with a full and sufficient Power to Treat with us for the Surrender of the said City of *London-Derry*, on reasonable conditions, they shall not after that time be admitted to any Treaty whatsoever; and the Army which shall continue the Siege, and will with the assistance of God soon reduce them, shall have orders to give no Quarter, or spare either Age or Sex in case they are taken by Force; but if they return to the Obedience due to their natural Prince, he promises them that the Conditions granted to them in His Majesties name, shall be inviolably observed by all His Majesties Subjects; and that he himself will have a care to protect them on all occasions, even to take their part, if any injury, contrary to agreement, should be done them, making himself responseable for the performance of the Conditions on which they shall agree to Surrender the said Place of *London-Derry* to the King. *Given under my hand this* 30th *of* June, *in the year of Lord* 1689. Le Mareshal de Rosen.

Col. Hamilton's *Proposals.*

I. THAT Col. *Oneil* has a Power to Vide Page 52. Discourse with the Governours of *Derry* from General *Hamilton*, as appears by his sending of this.

II. That the General has full Power, does appear by his Commission.

III.

III. That General *Rose* has no Power from
the King to intermeddle with what Lieutenant
General *Hamilton* does, as to the Siege, being
only sent to oppose the English Succour ; and
that all Conditions and Parlies is left to the said
Lieutenant General *Hamilton*: That as to what
Articles shall be agreed on, they may see by the
Kings Warrant he has full Power to confirm
them: Notwithstanding, if they do not think
this sufficient, he will give what other reasonable
Security they can demand. As to the English
Landing, such as had Commissions from the
Prince of *Orange,* need not be apprehensive,
since it will be the Kings Interest to take as much
care of his Protestant Subjects, as of any other,
he making no distinction of Religion.

IV. As to what concerns the *Inneskillin* People,
they shall have the same Terms as those of *Derry,*
on their Submission, the King being willing to
shew Mercy to all his Subjects, and quiet his
Kingdoms.

V. That the Lieutenant General desires no
better, than having it communicated to all the
Garrison ; he being willing to employ such as
will freely swear to serve his Majesty faithfully ;
and all such as have a desire to live in Town,
shall have Protection, and free Liberty of Goods
and Religion.

As to the Last Point, Such as have a mind to
return to their Homes, shall have a necessary
Guard with them to their respective Habitations,
and Victuals to supply them ; where they shall
be restored to all they possess'd formerly, not
only by the Sheriffs and Justices of the Peace,
but also by Governours and Officers of the Army,
who

who from time to time will do them right, and
give them Reprisals of Cattle from such as have
taken them to the Mountains.

At the Camp at Derry,
27 June, 89.   *Rich. Hamilton.*

---

*An Account of Officers Killed and Taken by the
Besieged in* London-Derry *during the Siege in*
1689, *whose Names we could learn.*

At Penny-burn-Mill.

General *Mommune* a Frenchman
Major *Tafe*
Major *Waggun*
Major General *Pusinan*   } Kill'd.
Capt. *Fitzgerald*
Quartermaster *Cassore* a Frenchman.

At the Windmil, May *the* 6th.

Brigadeer General *Ramsey*
Capt. *Fleaming*
Capt. *Fox*
Lieutenant *Welch*
Lieutenant *Kelly*   } Kill'd.
Ensign *Kadel*
Captain *Barnwel*
Ensign *Barnwel*

Prisoners

Sir *George Aylmer*
Lieutenant Colonel *Talbot*
Lieutenant *Netervel*   } Prisoners.
Lieutenant *Newcomen*

At

At the Windmill, June *the* 4*th.*

Lieutenant Colonel *Farwel* \
Two French Captains \
Adjutant *Fahey* \
Quartermaster *Kelley* }Kill'd. \
Ensign *Noris* \
Capt. *Graham* \
Lieutenant *Burcke* \
Ensign *Arthor*

Prisoners at the same.

Captain *Butler*, Second Son to my Lord *Mount-gerret*, led on the Forlorn Hope of Horse.
Captain *Mac Donnell.*
Captain *Mac Donogh.*
Captain *Watson.*
Lieutenant *Eustice.*
Sergeant *Peggot.*
A French Lieutenant.

At the Attempt of the Walls, June 28.

A French Lieutenant Colonel \
Captain *Mac Carlie* \
Captain *O Breayen* }Kill'd. \
A French Captain \
An English Captain \
An English Lieutenant

Prisoners.

A Corporal and Private Centinel

Officers Killed in several Places about the Town.

Lieutenant *Fitz Patrick* in the Orchard on other side of the Walls.
Lieutenant *Con O Neal.*

Ensign

Ensign *Conelly* kill'd in a Boat, and 13 Prisoners taken.

Two Friers kill'd in their Habits in the same Orchard.

Ensign *Ambross* on the Mountains.

Lieutenant *Talbot* had his Arm shot off at *Colmore*, from the Ships.

Drowned coming over at Liford.

Major *Nangle*.　　　　An Ensign.

Generals	1	Ensigns	6
Brigadeer Generals	1	Sargents	1
Major Generals	1	Corporals	1
Lieutenant Colonels	3	Cornets	1
Majors	5	Quartermasters	2
Captains	16	Adjutants	1
Lieutenants	9		
In all	48	And two Fryers.	

An Accompt of the Subsistance delivered to the Soldiers, and how many Companies and Regiments received.

Col. *Bakers*	25	Companies.
Col. *Walker*	15	
Col. *Crofton*	12	
Col. *Skiventon*	17	Col. *Michelbourn.*
Col. *Lance*	13	
Col. *Mount-ro*	13	
Col. *Hamill*	14	
Col. *Morea*	8	
In all	117	Companies.

Each

Each Company consisting of Sixty Men ; in all Seven thousand and twenty private Men, and Three hundred and fifty one Officers.

April 20. To each Company a Barrel of Beef, and a Boll of Meal. In all 117 Barrels of Beef, and 117 Bolls of Meal.

April 27. To each Man 4 pounds of Beef, and 4 quarts of Meal, and 3 pounds of Salmon. In all 21060 *l.* of Salmon, 28080 quarts of Meal, 28080 *l.* of Beef.

May 4. To each Company a Barrel of Beef, 120 *l.* of Meal, half a hundred weight of Butter. In all 107 Barrels of Beef, 14050 *l.* of Meal, 58½ hundreds and a half of Butter.

May 11. Six pounds of Meal for each private Man. In all 42020 *l.* of Meal.

May 18. Two pounds of Wheat to each Man. In all 14040 *l.*

May 24. Half a Barrel of Beef to each Company, 120 *l.* of Meal, half a Barrel of Barley. In all 58½ Barrels of Beef, 58½ Barrels of Barley, 14340 *l.* of Meal.

June 1. To each Regiment 5 Barrels of Wheat, and 5 Barrels of Shilling. In all 40 Barrels of Wheat, and 40 Barrels of Shilling.

June 8. One pound and a half of Meal to each Man, and half a Barrel of Barley to each Company. In all 9530 *l.* of Meal, of Barley 10530 *l.* of Wheat.

June 15. Half a Barrel of Barley to each Company, and a pound of Meal to each Man. In all 50½ Barrels of Barley, and 7020 *l.* of Meal.

June 19. One pound of Meal, and one pound
and

and half of Wheat to each Man. In all 7020 *l.*
of Meal.

June 21. One pound and a half of Wheat to each
Man.

June 25. One pound of Tallow to each Man,
one pound of Meal, and half a pound of Beef,
the Army consisting of 6185 Men.

July 4. Allowance to the Army being 5709
Men, to each Man one pound of Meal, one
pound of French Butter, and two pound of
Ginger, *per Com.* being 114 *l.* of Ginger.

July 8. To the Army being 5520 Men, to each
Man one pound of Meal, one pound of
French Butter, two pounds of Anniseeds, to each Company, being 114 *l.*
and one quarter of a pound of Tobacco.   Fry'd Tallow so call'd.

July 13. To the Army, consisting of
5334. to each man half a pound of
Meal, half a pound of Shilling, half a
pound of Beef.   Oats after grinding unsifted.

July 17. To the Army consisting of 5114, to
each man half a pound of Meal, half a pound
of Shilling, half a pound of Tallow, 3 pound
of salt Hides.

July 22. The Army being 4973, to each half a
pound of Starch, a quarter of a pound of
Tallow, one pound of Anniseeds, to a Company, being 117.

July 25. The Army being 4892. half a pound of
Tallow, half a pound of Shilling, three quarters
of a pound of Dry Hides.

July 27. The Army being 4456 Men, to each
Man half a pound of Meal, one pound and an
half of Horse-flesh, with two pecks of Bay
Salt

Salt to each Company, being an 117 Companies.

July 30. The Army being 4508 Men, to each man 3 pound of Meal, 2 pound of Beef, one pint of Pease.

May 5. To the Officers of Mr. *Skiventon's* Regiment, 4 Barrels of Beef, 4 Barrels of Meal, 4 Firkins of Butter.

May 15. To Colonel *Mountro's* Officers 4 pound of Beef, 3 pound of Salmon, 4 pound of Meal to each Officer.

May 25. Colonel *Hamill's* Officers one Firkin of Butter.

July 5. To 288 Officers, to each 2 pound of Meal, and 2 pound of Salmon.

July 13. To 351 Officers, to each 2 pound of Meal, and one pound and a half of Butter.

July 23. To 300 Officers, to each one pound of Wheat, one pound of Groats.

July 16. To 260 Officers, to each half a pound of Tobacco.

July 27. To each Officer one pound and a half of Horse-flesh, one pound and a half of Barley, being 252 Officers.

The Names of the thirteen Apprentices who closed the Gates.

Henry Campsie.	James Stewart.
William Crookshanks.	Robert Morrison.
Robert Sherrard.	Samuel Hunt.
Daniel Shorrard.	James Spike.
Alexander Cunningham.	William Cairnes.
John Cunningham.	Samuel Harvey.
Alexander Irwin.	

The Names of the Clergy-men that stayed in London-Derry *during the Siege*, 1689.

Mr. *G. Walker* Governor of *London-Derry* ⎫
Mr. *Mich. Clenakan* Minister of the same
Mr. *Seth Whittel of Bellioghy*, dead
Mr. *James Watmough* of *Arigal*, dead ⎬ Of the Diocess of *Derry*.
Mr. *John Rowen* of *Belteagh*, dead
Mr. *Rich. Crowther*, Curat of *Comber*, dead
Mr. *Tho. Sempel* Curat of *Donaghmore*
Mr. *Robert Morgan* Curat of *Cappy* ⎭

Mr. *Christ. Jinny* Prebend of *Mullah-bracke* ⎫
Mr. *John Campbel* of *Segoe*
Mr. *Moses Davies* of *Stewart* Town ⎬ Of the Diocess of *Armah*.
Mr. *Andrew Robison* of *Stewar* Town
Mr. *Bartholomew Black* Curat of *Aghalon*
Mr. *Ellinsworth*, from besides *Newry*, dead ⎭

Mr. *John Knox* Minister of *Glascogh*, &c. ⎫
Mr. ___ *Johnson* of ⎬ Of the Diocess of *Clogher*.
Mr. *Christy* Curat of *Monaghan* ⎭

Mr. *William Cunningham* of *Killishondra* in the Diocess of *Kilmore*.

As

As also Nonconforming Ministers to the Number of Seven, whose Names I cannot learn, four of which dyed in the Siege.

The Number of Bombs thrown into the City of London-Derry, since the beginning of the Siege.

	Big.	Small.						Big.	Small.
April 24.	...	3	*June* 28.			...		22	
April 25.	...	3	*June* 29.			...		10	
April 27.	...	18	*July*	2.		...			22
From *April* the 27th			*July*	3.		...			28
till the 4th of *May*,			*July*	4.		...		14	
at several times ...		6	*July*	5.		...		3	6
June 2.	... 3	1	*July*	6.		...		5	10
June 3.	...28		*July*	7.		...			18
June 4.	...37		*July*	8. and tenth					24
June 5.	...22		*July*	11.		...			4
June 6.	...30		*July*	14.		...			18
June 7.	... 6		*July*	15.		...			24
June 8.	...36		*July*	16.		...			16
June 11.	...	28	*July*	17.		...			14
June 13.	...26		*July*	18.		...			12
June 21.	...	21	*July*	19.		...			22
June 24.	... 6		*July*	21. 28		...			28
June 27.	...13							261	326
						Total		587	

Till the 22th of *July*.

Memorandum that one of the great Bombs being brought to the Scale did weigh 272 *l.* after 17 *l.* of pouder was emptied out of it.

And that one of the smallest Bombs being emptied, did weigh 34 *l.*

July

July 22.   42 Cannon Ball thrown into the City
about 20 *l.* weight a piece, before nine of the
Clock in the Morning.
More, 6 the same Evening.

July 23.   20 more before Dinner, and we could
not compute them afterwards, they came so
thick upon us.

A Letter writ by an Iniskellin-*Man, about the
Wrong done my Lord* Kingston, *by drawing
him from his Garrison at* Sligo, *to one at*
Derry.

S I R,

HAving this opportunity, I think ^{Page 20.}
fit to let you know the great and
most lamentable disappointment we are
under.   My Lord *Kingston* is basely us'd by
your Officers ; they have drawn him from the
Garrison of *Sligo,* which he had so bravely
Fortify'd, and had such a number of Disciplin'd Men both Horse and Foot in, and so
well arm'd, that he could not but have done
Service with them, and have made good that
Post against the Enemy : But Col. *Londy*
writ to him, That the Blood of all the Protestants of the North will lie upon him, if he
does not quit the Garrison of *Sligo,* and come
to their Assistance.   Upon this he marches
from *Sligo.* and at *Balishanny* meets a Letter

of

of Col. *Londy*'s, telling him, There was no
Provision for him at *Derry*, and that he must
quarter there. My Lord takes Horse, rides
twenty Miles in the Night to understand the
meaning of these things, but finds the Enemy
had stop't all passages to *Derry;* so he
returns to his Men, and there finds that *Sligo*
was possessed also by the Enemy. You may
imagine what a Distraction we were in upon
this; but with the most earnest entreaty we
prevailed with my Lord to go for *England,* to
solicit for Relief from thence, and are
resolv'd to take our shelter in *Iniskellin;* if
any thing happen amiss to us, our Children,
if they survive may curse your Great Men
for it, *&c.*

F I N I S.

THE SIEGE OF DERRY.

BY MRS. C. F. ALEXANDER.

"Oн, my daughter ! lead me forth to the bastion on the north,
  Let me see the water running from the green hills of Tyrone,
Where the woods of Montjoy quiver above the changeful river,
  And the silver trout lies hidden in the pools that I have
    known.

" There I wooed your mother, dear ! in the days that are so
    near
  To the old man who lies dying in this sore beleaguered
    place ;
For time's long years may sever, but love, that liveth ever,
  Calls back the early rapture—lights again the angel face.

" Ah, well ! she lieth still on our well-engirdled hill,
  Our own Cathedral holds her till God shall call His dead ;
And the psalter's swell and wailing, and the cannon's loud
    assailing,
  And the preacher's voice and blessing, pass unheeded o'er
    her head.

"'Twas the Lord who gave the word when His people drew
    the sword
For the freedom of the present, for the future that awaits.
O child ! thou must remember that bleak day in December
  When the 'Prentice Boys of Derry rose up and shut the
    Gates.

" There was tumult in the street, and a rush of many feet—
  There was discord in the Council, and Lundy turned to fly :
For the man had no assurance of Ulstermen's endurance,
  Nor the strength of him who trusted in the arm of God
    Most High.

' These limbs, that now are weak, were strong then, and thy
    cheek
  Held roses that were red as any rose in June—
That now are wan, my daughter ! as the light on the Foyle
    water,
  When all the sea and all the land are white beneath the
    moon.
                              " Then

"Then the foemen gathered fast—we could see them marching
    past—
    The Irish from his barren hills, the Frenchman from his
    wars,
With their banners bravely beaming, and to our eyes their
    seeming
    Was fearful as a locust band, and countless as the stars.

"And they bound us with a cord from the harbour to the ford,
    And they raked us with their cannon, and sallying was hot;
But our trust was still unshaken, though Culmore fort was
    taken,
    And they wrote our men a letter, and they sent it in a shot.

"They were soft words that they spoke, how we need not fear
    their yoke,
    And they pleaded by our homesteads, and by our children
    small,
And our women fair and tender; but we answer'd 'No
    surrender!'
    And we called on God Almighty, and we went to man the
    wall.

"There was wrath in the French camp; we could hear their
    captains stamp,
    And Rosen, with his hand on his cross'd hilt, swore
That little town of Derry, not a league from Culmore ferry,
    Should lie a heap of ashes on the Foyle's green shore.

"Like a falcon on her perch, our fair Cathedral Church
    Above the tide-vext river looks eastward from the bay—
Dear namesake of St. Columb, and each morning, sweet and
    solemn,
    The bells, through all the tumult, have call'd us in to pray.

"Our leader speaks the prayer—the captains all are there—
    His deep voice never falters, though his look be sad and
    grave,
On the women's pallid faces, and the soldiers in their places,
    And the stones above our brothers that lie buried in the nave.

"They are closing round us still by the river; on the hill
    You can see the white pavilions round the standard of their
    chief;
But the Lord is up in Heaven, though the chances are uneven,
    Though the boom is in the river whence we look'd for our
    relief.

                                                        "And

"And the faint hope dies away at the close of each long day,
  As we see the eyes grow lustreless, the pulses beating low;
As we see our children languish—was ever martyr's anguish,
  At the stake or in the dungeon, like this anguish that we
    know?

"With the foemen's closing line, while the English make no
    sign,
  And the daily lessening ration, and the fall of staggering
    feet,
And the wailing low and fearful, and the women stern and
    tearful,
  Speaking bravely to their husbands and their lovers in the
    street.

"There was trouble in the air when we met this day for
    prayer,
  And the joyous July morning was heavy in our eyes;
Our arms were by the altar as we sang aloud the Psalter,
  And listen'd in the pauses for the enemy's surprise.

"'Praise the Lord God in the height, for the glory of His
    might!'
  It ran along the arches and it went out to the town:
'In His strength he hath risen, He hath loos'd the souls in
    prison,
  The wrong'd one he hath righted, and raised the fallen-
    down.'

"And the preacher's voice was bold, as he rose up then and
    told,
  Of the triumphs of the righteous, of the patience of the
    saints,
And the hope of God's assistance, and the greatness of
    resistance,
  Of the trust that never wearies and the heart that never
    faints.

   .   .   .   .

"Where the river joins the brine, canst thou see the ships in
    line?
  And the plenty of our craving, just beyond the cruel boom?
Through the dark mist of the firing canst thou see the masts
    aspiring?
  Dost thou think of one who loves thee on that ship amidst
    the gloom?"

                                              She

She was weary, she was wan, but she climbed the rampart on,
 And she looked along the water where the good ships lay
  afar—
" Oh ! I see on either border their cannon ranged in order,
 And the boom across the river, and the waiting men-of-war.

" There's death in every hand that holds a lighted brand,
 But the gallant little *Montjoy* comes bravely to the front.
Now, God of Battles, hear us ! let that good ship draw near us.
 Ah ! the brands are at the touch-holes—will she bear the
  cannon's brunt ?

" She makes a forward dash. Hark, hark ! the thunder crash !
 O, Father, they have caught her—she is lying on the shore.
Another crash like thunder—will it tear her ribs asunder ?
 No, no ! the shot has freed her—she is floating on once more.

" She pushes her white sail through the bullets' leaden hail,
 Now blessings on her captain and on her seamen bold.
Crash ! crash ! the boom is broken ; I can see my true love's
  token—
 A lily in his bonnet, a lily all of gold.

" She sails up to the town, like a queen in a white gown ;
 Red golden are her lilies, true gold are all her men.
Now the *Phœnix* follows after—I can hear the women's
  laughter,
 And the shouting of the soldiers, till the echoes ring again."

She has glided from the Wall, on her lover's breast to fall,
 As the white bird of the ocean drops down into the wave ;
And the bells are madly ringing, and a hundred voices singing,
 And the old man on the bastion has joined the triumph stave.

"Sing ye praises through the land : the Lord with His right
  hand,
 With His mighty arm hath gotten Himself the victory now.
He hath scattered their forces, both the rider and their horses.
 There is none that fighteth for us, O God ! but only Thou."

And of these heroic times, if the tale be told in rhymes,
 When the statesman of the future learns no lesson from the
  past ;
When rude hands are upsetting, and cold hearts are forgetting,
 And faction sways the Senate, and faith is overcast ;
          Then

Then these Derry men shall tell—who would serve his country
    well,
  Must be strong in his conviction and valiant in his deed,
Must be patient in enduring, and determined in securing
  The liberty to serve his God, the freedom of his creed.

[The Publisher thanks the Proprietors of *The National Review*
for permission to print Mrs. Alexander's poem, "The Siege
of Derry."]

www.ingramcontent.com/pod-product-compliance
Lightning Source LLC
LaVergne TN
LVHW051748080426
835511LV00018B/3266